From Oatcakes to Caviar

Roy Smith

Published by

Corner House Publishing

Burslem, England

Printed in Great Britain by

Bookprinting UK

ISBN 978-0-9551053-2-6

Acknowledgements

Acknowledgements and my grateful thanks are due to the following, who helped me to produce this book.

I am deeply grateful to those at Room in the Roof Writers Group who put me on the right path when I started to write this book. I am also indebted to all those at City Voices Writers Group who have helped and encouraged me to overcome my inhibitions.

My thanks also to Jan Ryan, who designed the book cover, it was a difficult decision as to what to use to illustrate what I have put in words. Jan worked from my photographs to produce exactly what I had in mind.

My special thanks go's to Alan Barnett and his wife Maria for correcting my grammar and spelling, and for being able to read my writing!

Putting it into book form could not have been easy, as my writing has no full stops, comma's paragraphs or even chapters. When I write it is like driving a car on the motorway with my foot on the accelerator, there are no halt signs or traffic lights, I only stop when I see my children and grandchildren coming up the drive.

I have travelled all over the world and worked with some wonderful people under very difficult circumstances. I would like them to know that I am proud of all of them. I may not have mentioned them all in this book, but they will be forever in my heart and memories, and will never be forgotten.

For Joyce

Introduction

I first met Roy Smith in 2009, when he, looking totally bewildered, wandered into a meeting of Room in the Roof Writers Group, with the hope of finding some kind of inspiration.

Under his arm was a folder, it contained a host of facts and figures, dates and names, and was, to all intense and purposes a history of his working life. Sometime later, Roy, still looking puzzled, listened as members of the group explained to him how to structure and present his story in book form. They told him to cut out all the irrelevant details, as his story was being swamped by unnecessary clutter, and was already strong in its own right.

As I listened to Roy's story I was intrigued by the contents. Rather than name dropping, and there are plenty of names in the book to drop, Roy has managed to tell his story in simple terms, in his own style, with his own slant on an exciting and varied career. It is the story of an ordinary man, who has seen and experienced more than most of us could only dream of.

There have been low points in his life, like the passing of his wife, and his prolonged absences away from home when she was ill. Not that Roy was a workaholic, his family always came first, and he endured the time away from them with great anguish. He was, and still is a family man, but when he talks about his working life he speaks of it with great affection. The changes he has made to people's lives have been inspiring, and he always looks back on the many projects he has undertaking as a 'job well done.' Roy is a quiet and unassuming man and will only talk of his exploits when prompted.

He has taken this opportunity to put into words what his working life has meant to him. He has met many famous people, and all are documented here. He sees the publishing of this book as a chance to inspire others to put pen to paper. Roy has become a good friend to both myself and my wife. He is still just an ordinary man, or to put it in the words of the author himself *'just a hairy arsed bricklayer.'*

Alan Barnett

Corner House Publishing

Contents

Why?

This book has been written to make people aware of the poverty and starvation in under-developed countries. This is the twenty first Century and we still say 'charity begins at home.' When you work in circumstances which appalled me at the time, I realised what a horrible saying it is. Whilst I was working in Africa and seeing the poverty people experienced, and comparing them to the people in this country 'On the bread line,' as it is called I realised that those in this country were millionaires compared to those in Africa. I have had a long time to reflect on these events and it has greatly affected my thinking.

Media reports don't always reveal the full story – only what is sensational. Too often we give opinions after only reading a newspaper story, which is usually one side of events. We must make the media give us both, and do away with propaganda so we can then give an honest opinion.

The one thing people of all the countries I have worked in revere most about the 'wonder of the world' is our National Health Service, and yet we who live and work here treat it with indifference. Yes, there are things that go wrong, but if we are vigilant and reward 'whistle blowers' instead of punishing them we will be able to put things right. We are constantly learning, so let us admire it like other countries do.

Another thing we don't appreciate is Television, this is a wonderful way of educating people, and yet some countries do not allow it, as they feel it could cause riots as people see how others are living in the world.

So when we complain about some of the programmes we should remember we can switch to another channel or switch off. Some have not got the choice, as they are totally unaware of television's existence.

I have put my story into print so that when I am asked about my experiences I can provide documentary evidence in the written form.

The Early Years

I was born on the thirty first of October 1935 in Silverdale, a little village just outside Newcastle under Lyme, Staffordshire. I was the trouble that made my father and mother marry, and I was frequently told this during childhood.

Silverdale sounds an idyllic place to be born, yet the name is misleading, as this was a mining village. Many of its inhabitants were well versed in poverty, but like so many mining communities, families supported one another. Poverty often brings out rivalry between people which can be long lasting. It was in this village that I was born nearly seventy four years ago, but my stay was short lived, for after three years we moved to the next village of Knutton. This was an interesting place to grow up in, but not an easy one. It had a reputation for being rough and had many characters one in particular by the name of Chucker Jones comes to mind. Chucker was the local boxer, and always seemed to be involved in some trouble. He was well known to the local police. One event stands out well in my mind. Chucker had challenged another villager to a fight at a large shallow hollow where we played football and went by the name of 'The Whammy'. No-one seems to know where this name came from, but it was just the spot for Chucker and his opponent Ginger Needham to have a good old set to. News spread rapidly around the village that the fight was to take place, and of course in those days both young and old would gather to see such a spectacle. This gives an indication of the atmosphere in this village, for Chucker was not the only one to enjoy fighting. There were plenty of others willing to show off their prowess. Chucker though, was a name to be reckoned with, and one was not going to miss out on the entertainment. A large crowd, perhaps even two hundred, of which I was one, gathered at the Whammy and patiently awaited the arrival of the contestants.

 The fight was to start about 3 pm (the time the men left the various pubs) Chucker and Ginger had plied themselves with a large quantity of alcohol, although not from the same pub. At last the two contestants pushed their way through the crowd to the centre of the Whammy and faced each other, already swaying under the influence of their drinking, and began the contest. There was a vestige of organisation because a local man named Mr L...... offered to referee and keep time. After about fifteen minutes, with blooded faces from their noses and mouths, and looking a pretty frightening sight to me, a shout was heard, 'The Police are coming.' Of course knuckle fighting here had been illegal for some time and the local bobby, Constable Roper together with two more constables had been informed that the fight was to take place. People scattered very quickly to 'all points of the compass.' No-one wanted to be caught if the police were involved, because in those days they did not discriminate and even onlookers could be arrested.

Chucker and Ginger were last seen running off in the direction of Newcastle and therefore escaped arrest. What followed is uncertain but each fighter claimed that they had won.

Things at home were very difficult. Mother only had Four pounds Ten shillings a week from the army because my father was a soldier in the war. She had four children to rear myself aged five, my sister aged three and my twin brothers aged one year. So she was left with four small children when my father went off to war. Mother ruled us with a rod of iron, or rather a boiling stick. This was a spindled leg of an old chair used to prod the clothes around in the boiler. When we misbehaved, out would come the weapon and laid on us painfully. This was quite frequently applied, we never complained or hated her and we never held any malice against her, as we understood the hardship she had in feeding and clothing us. In fact I loved her very much.

One morning, sitting in the class at school there was such a commotion. Teachers running and hugging one another, shouting, 'The war is over!' I remember thinking 'thank God' he has answered my prayers, for every night we would pray for the safe return of my father. Little did I know what I was in for. He arrived later than the other fathers in the village as he was held back to load up all the tanks and ship them back home. This was because he was in the tank regiment.

Father looked suntanned and thin on his return and I did not remember him. The twins would not go near him. For a few weeks everything was fine, father had gone back to work at his old job. A company called Michelin, which was the local tyre manufacturer. Payday arrived, and mother asked for the housekeeping money. He grumbled and put four pounds on the table. Mother could not manage on that, so the rows started, and later out the boiler stick came, not for use on us children but on her. This was terrifying to us and we let him know it. However, being small children we ended up being beaten, this happened frequently with me, running up to the police station shouting to Bobby Roper, 'It's my father beating us again!' He was useless 'It's a domestic' he would say shaking his head. 'Now Reg, what have I told you about this?' It has got to stop' he would say to our father. Our neighbour Mrs Priestley would come out and shout at Roper, 'You will probably do something when he kills one of them and then it will be too late' But it made no difference, the beatings went on for years. We begged mother to leave him, but who would house her and her four children.

One time that made us happy (and God knows there were few!) was the village carnival.

There was a knock at the back door and the sound of it opening was accompanied by my Auntie Jean's voice.

'Edna, Edna, she yelled as she entered the kitchen are you entering any of the children in the carnival as there are some very good prizes?'

'No, mother answered, I've got no money to dress them in costumes, in fact I've got none at all because this little devil opened the front door to the rent man, and they all know better than to do that, only the rent man knocks at the front door everyone else comes round the back so I had to pay him.'

By now my other Auntie June, had come in explaining that they would dress us and it would not cost anything. She said that Doreen could put on an apron and a hair net and walk round holding a mop with a sign saying 'Mrs Mopp.' She told Mother that had a got a football strip and I could walk round with a ball with a number seven on my back.

By now everyone was talking and laughing apart from Doreen, my sister and myself.

'I'm not going' I shouted.

Auntie Jean reminded me that there were good prizes and even if I didn't win I could still have a bag of crisps and a bottle of Vimto all to myself. Auntie Jean could be very persuasive, and I thought to myself how I always had to share everything with my twin brothers and I could be on to a good thing here after all. I argued with her that my shirt was plain white and Stoke City had red stripes and in any case I hadn't got a proper football. She told me not to worry as she had some red paint and I could borrow a ball from the Y.M.C.A Club. Both her and Auntie June said they would be here next Saturday at 10 o'clock to get us ready and told mother it would not cost her a penny as they would see to everything. This was the first village carnival Knutton had know since the war and Auntie Jean was on the committee so she wanted her family to show some support. Sure enough, when Saturday came herself and June arrived with a ball and a tin of red paint. When I think about it now, I cannot believe I stood there in the back garden while June painted red stripes on my white shirt.

The carnival started outside the British Legion Club around the local Cenotaph, and there seemed to be thousands there so I did not feel afraid to walk around all the streets behind the Salvation Army band. The procession finished on the school playing fields, there was a stage erected on which sat the Mayor, his wife and all the local V.I.P's including Auntie Jean.

A man with a microphone called all the contestants up one at a time to the stage and instructed them to walk across and down the other side. The crowd clapped shouted and whistled to welcome us and once we were over the other side we were given a bag of Smith's crisps with a little blue packet of salt inside, a bottle of Vimto and a surprise gift which was a thin yellow thing that they called a banana.

It was the first time I had ever seen one, the twins would not bite into it they were so afraid, so I ate it myself.

It was now time for the awards and the winner of the fancy dress contestant was announced, and the winner was ....Stanley Matthews! Blimey, I thought, I will have to go on stage again to that man holding a small brown envelope. Eventually I got up there he shook my hand, gave me the envelope and ruffled my hair.

'Well, he said I had to vote for you, didn't I?'

Yes, it was the man himself, the maestro, my hero in the flesh....... Stanley Matthews.

This was the time when the seed entered my head to find out why some people are wealthy and famous and others not. I aimed to find out. It never bothered me to speak to famous or wealthy people after meeting Stanley Matthews, it came easy to me. My friends would always push me forward when we would go to the PMT (Potteries Motor Traction) Café on Saturday mornings. All the coaches would stop there on their way to all over the world, Like Bournemouth, Torquay, Newquay – well it was somewhere! I had no idea! Saturday was the best time to get famous footballers signatures on one page. I managed to get the Arsenal team players, like Joe Mercer, Leslie Compton, who then passed it on to his brother, who I think, did not want to sign it. He signed it Dennis Compton who besides playing football was a famous cricketer and a man named Alex Forbes with lots of wavy ginger hair also signed it. Georgie, my friend, said that that page was worth thousands of pounds and that we were very rich. When I told Mr Dalton, our sports teacher about them he was quite amazed when he saw it.

'What did they say when you asked for their autographs?' he asked. 'Nothing' I answered thinking why should they? That's how naïve I was.

The years rolled on, me hating my father and God. But I was getting older, bigger and stronger. I had finished with the Church and did not go again. I told the vicar about my father beating us, but he just ignored me so I did likewise.

It was only a matter of time before I would settle my account with father and it came when I was in the garden cutting the grass with a pair of cutters. There was screaming going on and terrible noises coming from the house, so I rushed in to find my father laying the stick on the backs of the twins. I could see the welds on their backs as they were both having a bath at the time and the water was red with blood. With all my might and strength I grappled with him. He went backwards falling down the side of the kitchen sink. Like an animal I jumped on him reigning blows around his face and head and shouting 'I want people to see what I've done to you' so every blow I struck was as hard and on his face as possible 'not like you hitting mother on her body so people would not see' I shouted. I remember seeing in his eyes that he was terrified. The only thing he could or would do was to bite my fingers, as I had by then got him by the throat. I had no doubt or fear that I was killing him. Then everything went black. After a few minutes a man in a black and white uniform was looking into my eyes saying,

'You'll be alright son!' It was the ambulance man.

My sister told me my mother had hit me on the head with the boiler stick. There was a doctor treating my brothers putting cream on their backs. I had a headache, which a cold water towel seemed to ease the throbbing. Roper as usual did nothing. Father had gone to bed and wanted nothing to do with them so everyone went home. It was a few days after when I saw him that he had two black eyes with lumps under both, a broken nose – plastered up, and his lips were very badly swollen. This did not bother me because I knew by the fear he showed me that there would be no more trouble and there wasn't, although it raised its head again many years later, when I married.

Father and I avoided one another for six years, never speaking, but unknown to me he was still hitting mother. Constable Roper came to see me. He told me that I was lucky not to be prosecuted. This gave me the opportunity to say what I'd been waiting to say for years. That I was only doing what he should have stopped years ago and that he was lucky that I didn't kill him – for that's what I wanted to do. I said that I would have liked to see what he and father would say in court as they were both cowards. He was white with temper but he said not a word and just walked away. 'Walk away like you always did!' shouted our neighbour, Mrs Priestley.

Two things that came to mind were seeing a pretty girl in the school playground, who became the major part of my life and the other was an incident that happened at Sunday school. Us boys used to have a game which was weeing up the toilet wall and the one who reached the highest won the game. Gibbo was the one who always won. He always won because he 'had the biggest penis' said John laughing. This may seem a silly game to the young of today but as the war was on there was nothing else to play with, so we made up games that did not need the expense of buying anything. These games included tick, rally oh! Hide and seek, and knocking on doors and running away. The next Sunday I thought I'd drink as much water as I could and hold it until we started the game, which is what I did. The wall, to my thoughts was about ten feet high. I was dying for my turn and just as I started the head of a teacher appeared over the top of the wall saying, 'What are you boys doing?' and then he started coughing and spluttering for I had let go and with much force hit him straight in the face. Well, I was in so much trouble, but I had at last become the champion pe'er.

'Factory fodder', is what you were called if you failed your eleven plus. How did I know this? Because during my last year at school I was made a prefect, having the duty of providing and serving the staff with tea, coffee and biscuits etc at break times. Many times teachers would come in saying, 'What's the use of trying to teach these children, they have nothing between their ears.'

They would say as one that we were only factory fodder. That saying haunted me, and I vowed never to work on a factory. To be fair the teachers were right it was true that 90% of the girls ended up working at Enderley Cotton Mills and others went to work at Rists and BTH or the Pottery Factories. The boys all followed or went down the pit or worked at Shelton Bar Steel Works. All this happened in the 1950's and even now watching modern day television there are programmes that show it is still going on as there are schools for the fodder and those for the privileged, but it is harder for the fodder because all the factories are closing but the privileged seemed to have no problems. They work hard at school and go to University and get jobs as Politicians and keep getting us into war after war. Others go into finance and banking and get the country bankrupt. What do the teachers say about failed eleven plus students now I ask? They call them army fodder, they go into the army and do what the privileged tell them to do and get themselves killed.

A Mr Field has done a survey of the dead in Afghanistan. His son was killed because he was not given the proper protective clothing which was supposed to be supplied by the privileged, and his findings only proves my suspicions. Of the 367 dead to date, only four came from the privileged class, the rest came from schools like mine. Mr Blair called for 'education, education, education.'

It makes one wonder what universities teach the privileged.

Why I tell this story is because I was favourite to become the head boy at my school but the headmaster who was also my Sunday school teacher voted for another boy and I became vice boy. I wonder why? This same headmaster Mr Beech, had sent for me to go to his room. Duly I went, and knocked on the door. 'Come in!' he shouted. In I went and there was sitting my mother. 'Oh dear' I thought what have I done now?' 'Smith, said the headmaster, 'tell us why you did not go to Wolstanton Grammar school on Saturday morning?

I had passed a written examination and Saturday morning was the oral and get together examination.

'I was playing football Sir' I replied 'We were playing the main rival school Orme boys and since I am captain'.........'

He interrupted, 'There Edna, what can I do? I do the best for him and he wants to play football'.

Mr Beech, (Fred to my mother) had both grown up together and had attended the same school, hence the familiarity.

At this time, I had begun to talk to the pretty girl in the playground, her name was Joyce. She said she knew who I was, as she knew my sister, they were in the same class. My courting had started and we ended up marrying on the third of November 1956. It was a church wedding, even though I had lost my faith in God years before. Church always reminds me of singing in Sunday School 'Jesus wants me for a sunbeam!' while my father was beating my mother at home. My little mind told me that something was not right.

Many years later, having a coffee in the Roebuck Centre in Newcastle, which was unusual for me, but this day I had decided to have a rest as my seventy years of age were beginning to tell on me. I heard a voice say 'Hiya Smithy' I looked behind me and there was quite a large man with a shaven head. He was smiling, I looked and stared and something told me I knew his face but could not put a name to it. 'You don't remember me do you?' he said, feeling embarrassed I said 'No'

'I'll give you a clue, I used to be the champion pisser'

'Gibbo' I said, shaking his hand. 'It must be fifty years since I saw you.'

'I've seen you a few times, he said,' I live at the top end of Clayton and spotted you when I've been on the bus, and my son Mark went to the same school as your eldest daughter Julie and he told me all about you and your travels.'

We spent hours talking having more drinks of coffee in case the lady would ask us to leave. We arranged to meet there again the next week at the same time. When I got home I could not wait to tell Julie about my meeting.

'Oh you don't know as you were working abroad' she said, but Mark who was a motorcycle policeman committed suicide, shot himself in the head with a double barrel shot gun. He was having affairs with other women. This made his mother very ill and she died later'.

Oh dear, I thought, Gibbo never said a word. Perhaps he thought I knew. We met regularly after that, and other widowers began to join us. Amphy and Waggy, two lads I played football with. Roman and Sid, were another two who sometimes we would meet at the local football matches where my son played.

'You'll never be as good as your father they used to shout at him.' Jeremy would smile at me and put two fingers up to Waggy.

I had become a professional mourner. One old mate I see at these funerals named Arthur said to me last time we met 'Roy, the way things are going there'll be nobody at our funerals!' 'Well Arthur, I said, 'If you come to mine, I'll come to yours.' I expected a roar of laughter, but Arthur looked at me and just said 'okay' with a smile on his face.

Work

I wanted to be a footballer. Mr Turner, a scout from Stoke City Football club asked my father to sign forms, but he refused, saying I had to have an apprenticeship to get a trade. My first working Christmas was 1950 I had just started work as an apprentice bricklayer for G A Poole. He sent me to Keele University on a site of houses for professors and lecturers. The general foreman was named Mr Jim Weatherhogg and he put me doing menial work around the offices, much to my dismay, for I wanted to lay bricks with the bricklayers. After a few weeks repeating my desire to lay bricks he said that after Christmas I could. I was told that an initiation ceremony was required before starting, it was something I was not happy about. On my first day I was grabbed by the men and they took off my trousers and painted my private parts with white gloss paint.

'Argh!' said Gibbo, when he heard. 'You would be different they painted mine in white undercoat.' Another joke was sending me to the ironmonger for sky hooks. Yes, I suppose we all go through these ceremonies.

Mr. Weatherhogg was always talking about Christmas dinner they were going to have chicken with all the trimmings. Chicken was a meat you only had at Christmas, my children find this hard to believe as you can have it every day now but after the war it was not possible. A couple of days before breaking up for Christmas Mr Weatherhogg was doing repairs under his estate car. It was made of wood, unbelievable but true, only at the back end though. There was a yell of pain, the jack had slipped and the car had collapsed on top of him. Men came running and managed to lift the car off him and an ambulance was called and he was taken to hospital. We restarted work after Christmas on the 4th January 1951 and who should arrive in his wooden car but Mr Weatherhogg. I was shocked as I thought he would still be in hospital. He looked strange, but I did not know what was up with him until he spoke.

'A cup of tea young un' he said, speaking through his teeth.

He had broken his jaw and had been wired up, there was no chicken for him now only what would go through a straw. We could not stop laughing, he turned to me and said through clenched teeth.

'After that cup of tea get your trowel out and go with the bricklayers,' and that's how I started to lay bricks. I worked under him for six years at Keele and for many years kept in touch until he died in 1999. I would like to think he was proud of me and people say he was. I certainly was of him, he was very proud of his service in the war, he was a Chindit in Burma, one of the many unsung hero's. I remember a man coming onto the site one day asking for a job and he was told there were no vacancies. When the boss came out of the office he looked at the man and said, 'Burma Jack?'

'Yes Sir' he replied.

They hugged one another and the boss told him there was a job for him here. Jack was very talkative and told us many tales about Burma whereas the boss never did. When anyone ever complained Burma Jack always came up with the same saying,

'It's not as bad as a Jap sticking a bayonet up your backside, you running to get rid of it, and him, running after you to give you some more.'

But one thing that happened which I have never forgotten and became quite a famous saying in the building trade, was when the building trade went on strike. We, not being in a union, carried on working, thinking no-one would see us, when one day a coach full of Liverpool men stopped, got out of the coach and started shouting 'SCABS!' I was laying bricks on the top scaffold when a man shouted.

'Hey, you hairy arsed bricklayer, come down 'ere', which we duly did, as these men looked very angry and fierce. 'Don't you know there's a bloody strike on?'

'Well, I'm not in a union,' I said. 'Well, you'd better bloody well join then, you hairy arsed bricklayers!' one said.

We duly did.

Many years later I recognised this man as Ricky Tomlinson the television actor. I would love to talk to him about this incident to confirm it, as we heard later that the police had arrested five Liverpool men in Shrewsbury for fighting and causing an affray. They all went to prison. The trial was on the television and they called them the 'Shrewsbury five' and Ricky Tomlinson was regarded as the ring leader.

I love telling the story about being at Keele University for six years. Oh yes, but I did not tell them about the building of it not attending it! When my eldest grandson and cousins show me their photographs of when they graduated with their mortar boards on their heads. I always tell them I have a number of those mortar boards – they look in disbelief, but I have neglected to tell them that a man kept putting cement on them! Perhaps you would have to be in the building trade to appreciate this story.

Returning to the yard after the Liverpool strikers left, we asked to see Mr Poole and told him what had happened.

'I've been expecting this but it's up to you guys if you want to work go to Freddy Bishop at Bignall End, he's in charge of building a Methodist chapel, it's out of the way, but you'll be alright there'.

I decided to go, as I had just bought a Royal Enfield motorbike and had monthly payments to make, although I had heard of bad reports about this man in charge. His nickname was 'The Poison Dwarf.' I started the next day and was pleasantly surprised, although I noticed that Freddy had a sarcastic manner, he never bothered me. One afternoon I heard a commotion and heard one bricklayer shout.

'You're not big enough to talk like that to me, F... off!'

Freddy turned and to my amazement got two bricks and stood on them. 'Am I big enough now George?' 'Yes' he said, and punched him right between the eyes. Blood poured from his nose and down his face.

'You are sacked and I am going to take you to court!' 'Go away you silly man, Mr Poole set me on and Mr Poole will sack me.' 'Right we'll see about that' he said.

Holding his handkerchief to his nose he got into his car and drove off.

'Carry on working lads, don't stop work, it's nothing to do with you,' we were told, so we carried on in amazement. 'What was all that about?' I asked Jack, another bricklayer I was working with. 'Have you smelled anything when George is near you?' he asked.

'Yes, I said, but being in the country and with a farm down the road I thought they were spreading sewage on the fields and now and then the wind blew this way.'

'Oh no, he said, it's George's feet, they smell horrible, that's why they call him sweaty fat George, but behind his back mind,' but Freddy didn't.

All this time I had been attending building college, passing my City and Guilds and doing two nights a week at night school. Doing these things deferred me from going in the army doing National Service for two years, but at the age of twenty one it was time to go in, although Mr Knapper, principal at the college had recommended me to go to Salford University for another two years again being deferred from National Service. I realised that I needed to go in and get it over with so that I could settle down and get married. Although I enjoyed the experience in the army this decision may have been wrong because after twelve months National Service was cancelled. If I had gone to Salford I would not have done my two years in the army. However, that is hindsight and it is how life treats you from time to time.

Work after the army was very different as Mr Poole was closing down the firm. Most of his men had left. He was getting old and tired of the building trade and his son was not interested in carrying on, so I moved around 'following the money' as they say. Firms like Wimpey's, Laing's you name it I worked for them from a hairy arsed bricklayer to site agent/engineer.

By this time my wife was about to give birth to our second daughter, much more easily than giving birth to Julie, our first. This was sheer panic, phoning the hospital, called Fanny Deakin's in Chesterton, saying that my wife was having very bad pains.

Fanny Deakin was a much loved midwife who lived in Silverdale, everyone within miles had known her. She was also a councillor and helped a lot of poor families, and God knows there were many. She was a Communist, which if you did not know her, would put you against her, as Communists had a bad name. As I have said, she was much loved in the North Staffs area so much so that they named the maternity hospital after her.

'Is it a fast baby?' a nurse said in a broad Scottish accent,'

Oh, I don't know,' I said nervously.

'You don't know if it's your fast baby? good God man, bring her in straight away.'

Getting her in the car and driving as fast as I could we arrived at the entrance, where we were met by a Sister. 'Are you the husband?' she asked, I nodded, 'and you don't know if it's your first baby?'

'First!'? I said, 'I thought you said fast.' I apologised.

'We've got one here!' she said to another nurse.

Later, when after nine years Joyce became pregnant again, much to our surprise, I drove to the hospital quite calmly, getting used to it by then.

The nurse told me to go to the waiting room and Joyce went down the corridor. In the waiting room were four men watching the television. 'Hi' I said, making myself comfortable, they nodded. After approximately fifteen minutes the door opened and the nurse shouted, 'You have a little girl, five pounds Mr Smith.' And shut the door.

I thought one of these other chaps must be named Smith too. Another fifteen minutes and the door opened again, the same nurse shouting 'you have a little boy four and a half pounds Mr Smith' and shut the door. We all looked at one another and I thought that someone would say his name was Smith, but no,

'My God!' I said, 'it must be me, am I the only Smith in the room?'

'Yes' they said looking anxious. One said 'Bloody hell mate, you've got two'. One offered me a glass of water and they all congratulated me. Joyce was wonderful and the babies looked beautiful, but small, which worried me, but the nurse said not to be concerned, they were very lively twins – and have always been so.

It was now back to work, and a meeting with a well known bricklayer, by the name of Knocker Holland. What a character he was. If he was a bricklayer then I'm a Dutchman! My brother-in-law was in charge of building a factory in Chesterton and by this time I was a manager, and I got this position for him. One day, I was called onto his site to see how he was coping, I spotted Knocker building a brick corner. 'John, what's he doing?' I said, pointing to Knocker.

'He's just started, he said, 'they sent him from the Job Centre.'

'And he can go straight back,' I said, 'look what a mess that corner is, it's not plumb and each course is not level, let's have a word with him.'

'I've heard you, but I can take you to one worse than this' Knocker shouted.

'You'd better show me then' I replied, as Knocker started to walk around to the other corner. 'Bloody hell! It's bloody worse, who built that?'I said.

'I did' said Knocker, bold as brass. I looked at John my brother-in-law who didn't know whether to laugh or cry. I didn't go to his site again.

There are many tales about the building trade I could tell better than 'Auf wiedersehen Pet', but it would take a book by itself and by that time I was getting married and off to do my National Service.'Good luck Knocker'!

National Service and Marriage

I was Twenty one, and getting married a week later to my childhood sweetheart, the reason being that my father would not sign for me to get married before. One of the jokes at my wedding said by my best man Graham was reading a letter from Her Majesty the Queen, inviting me to two years in the army, free of charge and to report to Aldershot in two weeks time. But it was no joke. One week on honeymoon and then Joyce saw me off to Aldershot from Stoke station. Arriving at Euston station I had to cross over to Waterloo to catch the Aldershot train. When I went down to the underground it was like another world, I didn't have a clue what to do.

There were thousands, (to my thoughts) of people. Seeing a ticket man I asked him directions and he said to get a one shilling ticket and follow the yellow line, which I did, ending up on a platform with a sign saying Aldershot plus many other places. A train came in, the doors opened, I got in, and the doors closed, and off we went within seconds. Sitting there looking at the train map I counted five stations and then mine, but to my surprise it was another station. I panicked and asked the fellow next to me if he could help.

'Oh you came to the wrong side of the platform' he said, 'you should be going the other way'

Bloody hell! What a to do, I thought.

'Don't worry, he said, 'you can stay on here all day going round till you come to your station it just takes a bit longer this way'. Sure enough, after about twenty minutes the train arrived at Waterloo. Going up a large moving staircase I arrived at the top to see a large number of entrances with their destinations above. At last I came to gate number eight which said Aldershot. Thank god, I thought, one and a half hours wait. Whilst waiting I noticed a lot of other lads about my age with their cases so I guessed we were all going to the same place i.e the 'Army'.

I met up with a smart, straight backed fellow with a cockney accent.

'Are you going for National Service?' I said.

'Yes, Queen Elizabeth Barracks' he said, Royal Army Medical Corps, by the way, my name's Ollie, Ollie Reed', he said.

'And mine is Roy' I replied.

At Aldershot, we both got off, and a soldier was shouting,

'Anyone for Queen Elizabeth, jump on this lorry', which we did with a number of others. About 20 minutes later we arrived at the camp.

'Get in line at that door, and enter when called by the sergeant who will take all your particulars', another soldier bellowed at us.

Ollie was in front of me as we were going through, then he heard the sergeant keep saying 'how do you spell this?' Ollie turned to me and said

'They can't bleedin' spell, we'll have some fun here. Ollie was next, the sergeant shouted, 'Name?' Ollie spelt it out for him. The sergeant looked up at him and if looks could kill, Ollie was a dead man.

'Occupation?'

'Playboy,' said Ollie,

'Bloody play boy?' What's that?'

'It's a kind of actor Serge', said Ollie, laughing, but with no sound coming out of his mouth.

'You'll be a shitting actor by the time I've finished with you lad' said the sergeant.

'Next', the Sergeant shouted.

'The name's Roy Smith ...S.M.I.T.H' I said,

'You being bloody funny lad?' The sergeant screamed

Oliie nearly fell over. I thought that if I stayed with this fellow I was going to get into trouble but when we got into the barracks room his bed was next to mine, oh dear I thought, that's all I need. Looking back it was the most enjoyable two years of my life. Ollie became my best mate and I'd like to think I was his. Going through training and attending many courses like first aid and with Ollie I attended the intelligence course, why is beyond belief, but later it became very useful to me. The two years soon went, getting into trouble getting out of trouble seem to come natural to Ollie. But a head ace to our commanding officer, Captain Roger Bannister,

'It's a good job you are a fast runner Smith' he used to say.

 Playing football for the regiment and being picked for the army side kept me very fit, although I never once beat the captain, nobody ever did, and I often came second winning many trophies for the regiment in cross country races.

After eight weeks of training we were given a thirty six hour pass. This enabled us to go out of the camp and to go anywhere as long as we were back by Monday morning at 6 am for parade. I told Ollie that this did not give me enough time to go home. He told me to come with him to London for a night as we could stay at the Salvation Army Hostel or Nuffield Centre, as there were plenty of places for servicemen.

Dave Alps, who bedded the other side of the billet asked if he could come with us, and before we had chance to arrange things there were five of us. Come Saturday morning we managed to get a lift in the camp lorry who dropped us off at Fleet railway station which was the nearest to us at around three miles away. The next station was Aldershot and Ollie said we were better off at Fleet because at Aldershot we would spend all our time saluting bloody officers who were everywhere. After around ten minutes the train arrived and there was a rush for a seat. We walked quickly along the corridors looking into every compartment until we came to two men who were looking into one of the compartments that contained only one man. We brushed them aside and rushed in.

'Come in boys sit yourselves down I see you are in the medics' said the little man sitting in the corner by the window.

I looked at this man, he was slim, with a very sharp featured face, long slim nose and ferret like eyes that were looking all over us.

'How do you like the army?' he said looking at me. I was getting worried, I know this man so be careful what you say Roy I thought.

'Well, it gets you fit, I've never felt so healthy this is our first pass and we are going to London for the night.'

The man then asked what I was before I went into the army. I told him I was a bricklayer and I had just serviced my apprenticeship and had only two weeks on full money.

He then asked me my name.

'Smith, Roy Smith Sir' I said.

'Ah Woy, do you know where that name comes from Woy?'

Then it hit me straightaway. I knew this man, I had heard him talking many times on the radio and television, he had a problem pronouncing his R's, it was Field Marshall Montgomery.

'No Sir I don't' I said.

He told me that in the first world war a lot of American's helped us, and some had the Christian name Roy, the most famous being Roy Rogers the cowboy, he told me that my father must have liked cowboy films, we all laughed.

He never stopped talking to us all the way to Waterloo. The lads could not understand me calling him Sir all the time. We walked along the platform at Waterloo. I told the lads who this man was as he now had two men with him one on each side of him. I told the lads it was Montgomery and we all came to attention as he passed us at he looked at us with a smile on his face. He stopped in front of me and said 'you are quite an alert fellow Woy, with good alertness and observation you will make a good soldier.' I thanked him and he carried on along the platform to be met by two red capped Sergeants.

I saw him many times but never had the pleasure to speak to him again. He lived in the next village Fareham, and he would walk to do some shopping and visit the Post Office but there were always reporters and photographers following him, as were the two men who I had brushed aside in the corridor on the train. As I have said, he was very talkative and was always asking questions and I have only wrote about

questions that were directed to me, which remembers me of my answer to him about being in the medics. My answer was that I was having a problem. Being a bit macho, I thought being a nurse, running about the ward with a bed pan or on the battlefield carrying a stretcher was not me.

'Well Woy, why did you join the medics?' he asked.

I told him I was playing football at the time and was told by the club to volunteer for the medics, as they had an agreement with them saying that if I played for the army on Wednesdays I would get a weekend pass, enabling me to go home and play for the club.

'Well, said Monty, you know it is very important being a medic, don't feel out of the action because the first thing a soldier shouts when wounded is 'medic', and when bullets and bombs are going off all around it takes a lot of courage to go to him with only a first aid kit, there are more medals given to these soldiers although it is only a small regiment.'

I had never thought of it that way but I told him I thought I would still prefer a rifle to a first aid kit. He told me that I would have to volunteer to join another regiment. He also said he was a socialist and was delighted when they got elected to run the country. I did not pay much attention to this although I was a little surprised as I thought he would have been a Conservative. It was later that I realised he, and many more in the army had voted against Churchill because

he was Conservative and they all agreed with Monty to have a change and all voted Socialist.

 After my two year service ended and moving back to Staffordshire I moved into a council flat and life began to be normal again. Only talking on the phone to Ollie reminded me of the army. One of my duties was to supervise the sergeant's mess, and one day on the menu was brown stew and dumplings to me this was the Potteries lobby and Barmy balls and when asked by the RSM what was on the menu I loudly said the latter. The RSM looked at me with a stern look until Sergeant Delucca explained about the Potteries food. He was a Potteries man from Hartshill. 'For God's sake Roy, don't put spotted Dick on for dessert'   Delucca said, laughing.

Ollie, myself, and Mumford and a couple of the lads used to sneak to the local pub called the Windmill and have a couple of pints if I remember. Ollie didn't drink, but came all the same, looking for girls. One night he did have a pint and the next morning on parade dropped one of his clangers. In the medics when you are given the order to number it was in fours. Ordinary regiments call their numbers one to how many there are in the line, for example there may be 40 in the line which meant the last man would shout 40. The medics would shout in fours, 1234, 1234, 1234, 5634. Ollie was not paying attention as he was number one and I number two, he shouted five I shouted six two, and of course the drill sergeant came looking at me thought it was me. So

he put his nose on my nose with such a stern face I started to laugh, until the RSM came into view, he quickly gave the order to number off and he stayed with me to make sure that it went right this time.

I've already said that Ollie would join in any courses going. One day he came to me with forms to be an officer.

'You must be joking, a commissioned officer?' no way' I said.

'Will you help me to fill in this form he said?'

'Yes I replied, and it was then that I realised, that Ollie had difficulty in reading and writing. We would now call it Dyslexia. Ollie was away about a couple of months and was back with three stripes.

'Not good enough' he said.

It was about this time we began to drift apart. I was into sport and Ollie was with his fellows who liked acting and was always putting on shows in the Naafi. There was only one show I joined in and this was the Black and White Minstrel Show. I had done this at school and like an idiot had told Ollie

Ollie was brilliant, and a new friend named Berry was also very good. Another time the RSM called me to tell me about another RSM who would be staying at the Mess and everybody especially me must see that he gets looked after.

'He's here for about four to six weeks and he is boxing for the commonwealth' said the RSM. His name was RSM Amin, a six foot African weighing about 26 stone. He was very pleasant, no problems at all, I found it difficult to have a conversation with him and I always asked him if he wanted to do this and that. I suppose years later, people had wished I had put a cyanide tablet in his morning coffee.

Around a couple of years later, Ollie rang me to say he was coming to the Potteries to look around. He wanted to see Burslem and the other towns, as he was reading Clayhanger, and he was hoping to get a part in it. He also wanted to visit Wedgwood and Doulton and to get a brown teapot for his Grandparents from a company called Sadlers. I told him I would pick him up at Stoke Station. He arrived on the Wednesday at 10.30 and after his usual greeting he told me he had not passed his driving test.

We went to Burslem, and he bought a figure from their shop in Nile Street and then we went over to Sadlers. I knew Peter Sadler, as I had done some building work there. Peter showed us around, showing us all the beautiful teapots, but Ollie said that his Gran wanted a brown one. These happened to be the cheapest, but I don't think this had anything to do with it, as it was what his Gran wanted.

I drove him to the Wedgwood shop, he bought a few items in blue and white china then I drove him through all the six towns, he said he had never seen anything like it, it was like

being in another world he said, and kept on about the toilets being outside. He said one thing that would get me the part would be talking like me, like a Quaker, with thee and thou and wut. We had a meal and a couple of pints in the North Stafford Hotel opposite the station then he caught the 6pm train and he made me promise to call on him in London at any time.

Cricket

Joining the self build group in Clayton bought my attention to the local cricket club, which was just around the corner, about 200 yards away. Knowing a few of the players from my football days I joined them. This brings to mind the day when I introduced the Rev. Peter Travis to the team in the dressing room. Mr. Molby was President of the club and he asked me to take Peter into the dressing room as he was the new opening bat. 'Oh dear I thought, I hoped the lads are not swearing which was frequently used by most of them 'Lads' I shouted, as I opened the door 'this is the Rev. Peter Travis.' putting a loud emphasis on the Rev.

 'Flipping heck!' Are you the new opening bat?' said the Brock,

 'Yes' said Peter, and carry on, it doesn't bother me, I've heard it all before' and we all laughed with relief. We were playing the top team Chell, who had a very fast West Indian bowler, 'get padded Tunnicliffe and Travis, we're batting first', said our Captain Barratt. I was not very happy with Barrett, and I asked him why I was number eight in the batting order. 'Because you're not good enough to be higher' he said sarcastically. Travis was facing the fast Gilly who was standing near the site screens. That's how long his run was to release the ball I never saw it, just Travis dropping his shoulders and the man on the boundary throwing it back. 'F.... F... Hell did you see that' said Brock, 'no' I said thinking whether I dare ask Barratt if I could go to number 11! Travis was batting beautifully, considering we had no helmets and

guards, only pads and gloves and not forgetting our manhood boxes. We got to double figures when Tunnicliffe was out, and losing another three wickets for a measly 30 runs. Travis scoring most of these, next one out and it was Brock's turn.

There was a strong smell, but he said it was OK, shrugging his shoulders, 'I'll sort him out' six runs more Brock walked out to cheers, as he was a favourite of the crowd. The first ball went past him before he moved his bat, shrugging his shoulders, patting the ground ready for the next ball he swung his bat and the ball hit it, four runs. Waving his bat to the crowd, 'Fetch that from the boundary Gilly!' shouted Brock. Gilly was getting angry and the next ball went very close to Brocks head which unnerved him. The last ball of the over was the 100 miles an hour ball and his wickets went everywhere.

'Fetch those bails back from the boundary' shouted Gilly.

Travis was very quiet, watching all this and trying very hard to keep Gilly away from the lower order. 'Roy you are next in' said Brock 'are you all right?' 'Yes' I said nervously, 'I asked Jean in the kitchen if I could borrow a Tampax?' And Brock turned to go before realizing it was a joke, but was it a joke? As I got into the wicket Peter came to me saying in his Yorkshire accent,

'Keep your bat and pads in front, protect your wicket, don't worry about LBW. This umpire will not give them' which I did

and Travis got the score to 70 and then he was out, a snick to slips. 'What shall I do now Peter?' I shouted.

'Pray!' shouted Peter. We were all out for 82 runs. Chell soon knocked the required runs although Brock and Fordy got three wickets a piece. What I enjoyed most in my cricket days was the camaraderie, having a social drink meeting friends every Saturday. Many years later I became big friends with Gilly in the West Indies, where I worked for a few years. He remembers the game very well and that I was the only one to answer the umpire, when asked what guard I required, I replied square leg. You would have to know your cricket to understand this joke.

As I said at the beginning, I joined a self build group, this came about as my brother, who is a plumber, and his friend Graham who was a Joiner, came to see me one night at my house in Silverdale. It was a council house given to me as I was on their list for two years when serving my National Service. This was an acceptable period for them. They had joined this group eight of them but the bricklayer had pulled out and they asked if I would be interested as they had bought the land which was in Clayton. Joyce seemed interested and I certainly was, I had always wanted to build

my own house. But we would like to see the land, which we did the following day.

'It's just right for the two girls' my wife said, 'schools close by, Newcastle just a walk down Clayton bank and a few local shops and a little children's playground next to the land'.

The other men seemed to be very agreeable so we accepted. We had to put £400 down to buy the plot and make a start. One thing quietly made me nervous, there were four joiners, one plumber, one buyer, one handyman so called, and me the only bricklayer. Could I on my own lay all these bricks for eight houses? I saw why the other bricklayers had withdrawn but I had told Joyce I would do it. It took three years, each year getting harder. The problem was as they were being finished people moved in, so that we could get their mortgage money of £800 to carry on building the others. But some of them stopped doing their share of work and even sold up and left with a tidy profit. Not even thanking us that were left.

My Brother Brian was having number eight, I was having number seven, and Graham was having number six so we had to carry most of the load. At times we were in despair, but we ploughed on. It was our own fault in a way, as we had picked them, me because it was the largest plot and backed onto the children's playground, which was a blessing for the children over the years. Brian was the last of the original eight who sold out for £26,000, not bad for £1200

working a few nights in the summer weekends, for three years. But myself, Graham and Alf, both joiners, have had the last laugh, the only three left of the eight and our properties are worth £200,000 plus now, not a bad profit for £1,200.

A few years later, when Joyce had the twins, I decided to join Staffordshire Public Works as a building and civil engineer. The money was very good and it included a new Ford Cortina estate just the thing for my family. There were a lot of responsibilities, but with hard work I overcame them. Eight years I stayed with them, my contract was mainly building construction, all the other engineers were civils, mainly dealing with the roads and sewers, motorway maintenance etc. If they came across any construction they passed it on to me. I made a lot of friends, which I still meet from time to time.

Mr. Pinfold our Chairman shocked us at a monthly meeting saying that he was selling out to a firm called the William Boulton Group from Burslem. I had heard a rumour, as they were my clients, anything they wanted to alter or extend I was the engineer they sent for. I knew their chairman Mr Fahey and MD Eric Birks very well as I had supervised work at their private homes. All but a handful would be made redundant as they only wanted to keep the mechanical section running, they had a good contract with JCB making steel buckets. I was one not to be made redundant and I

disliked doing odd jobs around the company's that Fahey owned. It was now near Christmas, and I looked forward to meeting all the engineers and friends that I had left as we had arranged a social night at the Plough Inn on Campbell Road. Joan had arranged it, as it was her father and mother who owned it. Joan worked in the wages office, and had seen to it that there was a very good buffet laid on. To everyone's amazement they all arrived. Three of the lads had gone to work overseas for a company named Alfa engineering in Holland. Mike had gone to Saudi to run a contract for them there. Mark had gone to Hong Kong fixing a monorail for the railways. Zed was in Poland for them working on the Warsaw Airport. They were all on twice the money I was on, and no tax. Accommodation and food expenses all paid for. The salary went in your account at the end of every month, no stoppages.

'Do you think I could do that?' I asked Joyce

'How long will you be away for?' she asked Mike. 'Twelve weeks' he said 'and then you have four weeks off paid 12 weeks', That's not long I thought. My brother had emigrated to Australia and suffered terribly with homesickness, would I be the same? 'They are desperate for someone like you who knows a bit about civil as well as construction, give them a ring, this is their address and phone number, I'll mention your name so if you call tell them Mike Comerford has recommended you,' he said

A few weeks after Christmas, after talking it over with Joyce, I decided to phone Alfa engineering. I was put through to a man called Demag. He said Mike mentioned me to him and would I come over for an interview, all expenses paid by the company. I said yes and it was arranged a day later. That same week I was being met at Sekipol Airport by a smart medium sized man with a black beard with Mr. Smith written on a plaque highlighted so that it could be seen.

'I'm Mr. Smith' I said. 'How do you do, my name is Demag, I'm the office manager and I'm to take you to the head office, it will take about half an hour by car. Have you got your C.V?' he said as we entered a beautiful reception area, 'you relax while I organize the meeting, Jan will bring you a coffee or tea, which would you like? I will not be long'.

'Right Roy we are ready,' he said showing me the door which took us into a large room with six people sitting around a large table. 'This is Mr. Smith' and introduced me to the M.D. Mr Rikham. Mr Prins, and Alan Walsh the only Englishman and others.

We've looked through your C.V' said Rikham and we all agree you are just what we require, is there anything you would like to know?'

'Yes' I said, 'what will be expected from me?' 'Well' Alan Walsh said. 'your experience in civils is useful but your construction in building is very important although we do not actually build we supervise the building to our requirements

as to fit in with our machinery, you will be working with the architects drawing the plans, these plans will all be the same no matter which country we are working in, the only difference will be language some are originally Dutch but others are English and Spanish.'

'it's important that you know these drawings off by heart, as sometimes they get lost and is used as an excuse if anything is wrong, I would say after a couple of months you would be ready for an overseas posting and I'm hoping that will be with me in Cuba.' The Salary and a contract was acceptable, it was only when could I start. This would be at the end of the month. Fahey was surprised but accepted it although no redundancy was forthcoming.

It was around this time when we were woken by someone banging on our front door at 2 o'clock in the morning.

'Who's that?' I asked Joyce, 'It's your brother Barry' she replied. 'Father has hit Mother and she's in hospital, will you come home, as I think we've killed Father.'

Barry was on his motorbike so I said I would follow in my car. At home Brian, my other brother was on top of Father holding him down with his foot on his throat, he was a bluish colour so I told Brian to take his foot off and the colour started to come back in his face

'A neighbour has taken mother to hospital, can you and Barry go and see if she's alright? I'll look after this bastard',

Brian said, and kicking father in the head at the same time. When we arrived at the accident ward mother was just getting ready to leave.

'Broken ribs, she said, they have strapped me up after the X rays and told me just to rest and take pain killers,' she said, thanking Mr. Lightfoot a neighbour. We took her home. As we arrived you could hear father shouting obscene language and screaming and then a bang, when he started to cry.

'What shall we do with him?' Barry said.

'I don't care', mother replied, 'put him in my car we'll take him to the Smiths, it's about time they knew what a bastard they have brought in this world.' So the twins got hold of him and after a lot of screaming and fighting, got him in the back seat. Every time he shouted, one of the twins punched him in the face. 'Shut up' they would say.

Banging on the front door of the Smiths, who lived in New Ashfields about two miles away, his sister Winnie opened the door where as we pushed father through to the passageway, shouting

'We have put up with this bastard for years, it's time you had a turn' closing the door shut, we got into the car and drove away.

'Tomorrow you can expect trouble, so stay with mother until I arrive, and we will have to arrange that someone is with her

at all times, I know you are all working, but we'll have to do something because I'm sure he'll be back' I said.

Sure enough he arrived with his mate. Bobby Roper opened the door which was bolted. 'No' shouted mother, 'But he has no clothes' pleaded Roper. After a few minutes Brian opened the bedroom window and threw out bags and clothes all over Roper and father, who were sitting on the lawn. Just at this time I arrived and, ignoring them, went around the back where Brian let me in, Roper was talking to mother all this time.

'He says it's his name on the rent book, how can that be, he's been in the army five years, did he send the rent to the council?' asked Roper. 'No I paid' mother shouted.

A car stopped and out came Winnie, and a man in a pin stripped suit carrying papers which he gave to Roper. 'This is a written warning that if your sons do anything like it again they will be arrested' shouted Roper, it has been handed to me by their solicitor',

'What use is that when for years we have pleaded with you to stop him from hitting mother and you have done nothing, so I suppose that letter is useless as well, we will gladly go to court if it stops this abuse.' I said.

Nobody replied, they all went away but father stayed sitting

on the lawn 'I'm sure something is wrong with him' Brian said

'Yes he's got Dehli belly' mother said 'what's that'?' Brian asked, looking at me. 'It's a disease the English soldiers contracted in India' I replied.

Later that night Roper returned with two more constables and they pushed the door open, father and his clothes went upstairs to his bedroom. I left, knowing the twins could look after mother and perhaps this would be the end of any more abuse. One year passed by and there were no further problems. Barry got married but it still left Brian to keep an eye on mother, we all looked in on her. The same thing happened again but it was Brian banging on the door shouting 'Dads died our kid' 'never' I replied. 'What's happened?'

'He came from The British Legion about eleven o' clock and collapsed on the settee, mother said he went white, so she called the doctor, who came out and said he'd had a heart attack, he tried to bring him around and gave him an injection, but after about an hour he gave up, saying he is very sorry but he is dead.'

At the funeral none of the Smiths attended, a few of his drinking pals from the British Legion were there, the rest

came from friends and relations from my mother's side, showing respect for my mother. He was forty eight years of age, and buried at Newcastle Cemetery, and in all the forty

four years, no one has ever put a flower on his grave, I should know, I only live about four hundred yards from the cemetery. The Smiths I found out recently, were a very secretive family, a man had called who was writing about the Captain of the Titanic and mother sent him away very rudely, so my sister told me, and when I opened a box of personal things of father's, I found photos of men with beards and post cards of ships one from the White Star line ship called Olympic, I'm sure it would have been of interest to the man.

Cuba

The phone rang 'Hello, Smith speaking,' I said. 'Hi Roy, Demag here, said a voice, just letting you know everything is arranged, so on Monday you are to go to Manchester Airport for 8.00am as your plane takes off 10.00am to Madrid where you will have approx four hours wait for the Cuban flight. At Manchester go to the K.L.M. Airways desk, identify yourself and they will hand over an envelope in which are your tickets, expenses, and information, plus a letter for Alan Walsh and technicians, who will meet you in Havana. 'Well Roy all the best hope everything goes alright for you,'

'Thank you Demag,' I said, and I'll see you in twelve weeks time at the Christmas party, cheers.'

Demag was the Office Manager for the company, I had been working for three months in Amsterdam, Holland as a building and civil engineer, travelling from Manchester, every Monday morning arriving Amsterdam at 8.00am there being picked up and driven to the office, returning to Manchester, Friday around 6.30pm.

Monday morning and my wife Joyce drove me to the airport with our four year old twins, which she had done for the last three months, only this time I was not going to Holland, but to Cuba for twelve weeks. My yearly contract was twelve weeks then four weeks leave (paid), so we were hoping it would soon go.

The flight to Madrid was good, there were no problems going into the transit area, I booked in at the Cuba flight desk, noticing that there was no time given on the above board, so I asked when it was due, the lady who took my ticket replied it was not known, but she said to keep my eye on the board. It was now 1:30 one hour in front of British time, four hours waiting, no sign of my flight, so I went to the desk, I noticed it had changed to K.L.M. I told the lady about my situation she told me that they had no information regards this flight and in her experience it arrived when it arrived, as Cuba was in conflict with Angola and impossible to keep to a timetable, but as soon as it arrived I would be sent for.

Feeling pretty tired and miserable realising there was nothing I could do but wait, I kept on looking at the check-in counter but all the lady could do was to shake her head in sympathy.

The airport was very quiet, so I lay down on one of the many sofas and went fast asleep, waking at 6:30am in a panic. When I looked at the check-in counters, they were all closed. I decided to go to the restaurant and have a coffee, buying an English paper to read while keeping my eye on the flight board. There was no movement, and at 8:00am the check-in counter opened. I saw the first lady when I arrived so I went to her, seeing that she was embarrassed, she said that she would see to it straight away, offering me a breakfast and lunch voucher and apologising that no one had offered me a night at the local hotel.

I had breakfast, then waited, had lunch and then waited, until my patience finally gave out. I told the lady that I wanted to take the next plane out whether it was Cuba or U.K. There was a flight to London at 5:00am, and I said that I would take that. One hour later the lady on the K.L.M. desk started to wave at me. Telling me my Cuban flight was on its way and would arrive at four thirty. She asked me what I wanted to do. I told her I would take the Cuba flight, but could she tell me where the other passengers are. 'AAH, she said 'there is only one besides you and he has not arrived but has been notified so I am expecting him anytime.' This was very strange, a plane coming just for two passengers, the other person must have been very important because it wasn't me.

Two armed airport police came to the check-in desk and the lady pointed to me.

'Senor, are you for the Cuba flight?' they asked.

'Yes' I said,

'Follow us we will escort you to the plane which is at the end of the runway, your luggage has been sent ahead.'

Walking across to the plane thinking I've never known this before. Walking to the end of the runway, I noticed a man in front of me in a smart black suit, this must be the important passenger I thought. At the bottom of the moveable stairs were two men, one in a smart uniform, he was a senior pilot, and two other men, one carrying my suitcases.

'Senor, are these your cases?' If so, will you check inside that everything is correct.'

Undoing my cases and looking in I found everything looked okay and said so, the other man had gone up to the door of the plane so I followed, noticing the handlers carrying my suitcases behind me. Entering the plane my cases went left to the flight deck and I turned to my right, talk about being surprised I froze in a state of shock. Never in my life had I seen such a sight, there must have been one hundred and sixty wounded soldiers all with bandaged heads, shoulders, arms, chest and legs, and where there should have been overhead racks there was a row on both sides of men laying in makeshift hammocks, all their bandages were blood stained.

They all had weapons of one sort and another, and now of course everything was beginning to click. The secrecy of the flight, surely this was not allowed? Worse was to come as my hostess took me to near the back of the plane, where there was one seat in between two soldiers. With difficulty, I managed to get up the gangway, the gangway being in the middle with three seats each side.

The soldier on my left looked very ill with a head wound, he never spoke a word. I think he was Cuban.

The soldier on my right was a black, he was pleasant and spoke a little English, he liked English football. I told him I came from Stoke, where Stanley Matthews came from, his eyes lit up.

'Stanley Matthews' he kept on saying until everybody on the plane knew.

The flight was eight hours of agony, with only one glass of water, one glass of orange, and a sort of fish sandwich with a piece of something in between that resembled a cross between pastry and sponge. Was I glad to land in Havana, the plane seemed to take hours to unload.

The passport hall was practically empty, but I did notice Liberian hostages sitting at the far side. I had filled my questionnaire form in and handed it to an official with my passport.

'Englease' he said fiercely, looking sarcastically at my passport, and then said, 'What's this religion?' (Church of England) shouting 'I suppose Jesus was an Englishman in your English Church' and threw them back at me landing on the floor.

The anger was rising in me, my fists became closed and my arms began to rise. One of the Liberian hostages must have seen I was having difficulty and came to me picking up my passport and form.

'Let me help you' she said.

Telling her what had happened, she pointed out where it said religion and told me to put Christian giving me another form, I filled it in as she had shown, handed it back to the Official with an angry look on my face that matched his. Though there were only a few people in the hall, the noise at times was deafening.

Collecting my suitcases, I made my way to the exit doors, as they opened the noise was coming from outside as there were crowds of people shaking hands, hugging and kissing all the wounded soldiers who had come out a different way. Again I froze, for only about four yards from me was Fidel Castro with his arms around the soldiers and hugging them. His eyes met mine, and I could see in his, were sorrow and tears. I had been brought up to look into someone's eyes to feel the truth.

So this was the horrible Dictator, the evil communist who the Politicians, media and Americans had told me about.

Dressed in cheap Khaki, with no bodyguards, I thought how easy it would be to kill him, but after looking around at all these people I realised that they loved him and it would be impossible to find anyone to do the deed.

'Roy, Roy' someone was on top of a VW mini bus shouting, it was Alan Walsh, a man came up to me, took my cases and said. 'Come Senor Roy'. I followed and eventually shook hands with Alan saying 'Thank God, at last'.

'Sorry about all this' Alan said, 'But when I heard they had booked you Cuba Airways I went mad, they know you should come by Liberia Airways, it is cheaper by half than Cuba so next time refuse' 'this is Raphael our driver and translator' said Alan, pointing to the chap who had carried my cases.

Later Raphael became my closest friend and helped me many times, and I would like him to think I helped him. The airport was about 15 minutes run from the house I was to live in, with three Dutch technicians, Ben, an electrical engineer, Sip a refrigerator engineer, and Cip who was a monorail technician, all four of us having a bedroom each. There was a lady cook, who was also a cleaner, as there was very little to cook with. Across the road was another house with three technicians, Moutan, Ronn, and John who were responsible for all materials and automatic machines. The contract was to supervise six slaughter factories this was called a Turn Key project as it involved setting out a site and construction of the many buildings. To do this we had to drill for water to build a generator house for electricity, build a tower to pump water into to give water pressure around the site, build and render a house to make use of waste such as feathers, feet, heads and innards of poultry and any other animals they would slaughter.

We also had to build the main factory that housed the monorail carrying the animals around to the machines, the first would give them an electric shock, the second would kill them by cutting their throats and then their heads off. Many machines had to be used depending on the kind of animal. The only one that involved human help was taking the innards out and waste. At the end of this process was a building attached, in which was the refrigeration plant, freezing and packaging. Finally a water treatment plant where all waste water was piped to and chemically treated to a standard eighty nine degrees pure water before being released into irrigation troughs on the fields. This was a constant thorn in my side, getting that eight nine degrees, and supervising all this. Unknowing to me, these factories had started two years before, Sip and Cip had been here all that time. By now we were speaking good Spanish. Alan the project manager had been here for one month and I could tell that Sip and Cip were calling the shots, and I realised why.

Alan insisted on an English engineer as his authority was in trouble with these two guys. Alan lived in the next avenue with his wife Yola and four year old son. This area was a special area for foreign people, being patrolled by the army keeping away women and undesirables. The estate had been built by very wealthy and famous people, the house we lived in belonged to Clark Cable, the British Ambassador was in Frank Sinatra's house, and the other houses belonged to Ava Gardner, George Raft, and many more famous people, but the most famous was Al Capone's, where the Dutch Ambassador lived. That night the lads invited me to go out to have a drink and a meal, but I declined as I was tired. I went to bed and slept like a log wakening up at 5:00am by a knock on the door, it was Ben telling me they were going to work, but Alan had told them not to take me as he had plans for me that day.

I had breakfast prepared by Ellana, of new bread, cheese and jam, 'funny jam this' I thought.

At 10:00am Alan walked in.

'Morning Roy feeling better?' he said.

'Yes much better, thank you', I replied.

'Would you like a coffee?'

'No I've had my breakfast,' he said 'but be careful with that jam, do you know what it is?'

'No' I said, 'but it isn't very nice'.

'It's bloody Caviar Roy, it's the nearest to jam we can get' he said laughing.

'It's plentiful and cheap, it comes from Russia.'

'We are going around some of the sites today' said Alan, the first is Los Benos, which is to be completed in three weeks time because this is most important to the Head Office in Holland in order to get the final payment'.

It was about fifteen minutes drive, with Raphael driving. We arrived at two large wired double gates, one soldier opened them and waved us through.

'They know us' said Alan.

I could see that all the construction was finished, roads were completed and the men were all inside but for a few, over at the offices. They were all dressed in the same dark denims, but some had a white stripe down the side of their trousers and others white rings around their tops, the rest were plain, and of course the soldiers were in light khaki uniforms, this was to identify crimes, the stripes were the dangerous ones, murderers etc, the rings are for Politicians, and people who were involved with Batista and carried out his wishes.

They had an option of being shot or twenty years imprisonment, but it was common knowledge the top ones were shot. The others are what we called minors, jailed for one to five years for stealing, or not working, fighting and small offences.

'Well what are they doing here and where are the workers?' I said.

Alan laughed and said,

'They *are* your workers, in Cuba there are no prisons, that's what building sites are, that's why the perimeters are all wired, and in each corner if you look up are towers with soldiers holding automatic weapons, there's very little trouble here'.

All the sites were the same, so one set of drawings did all of them, each site had a brigade, these were like your building companies e.g. Wimpey, Laings, Barratts, etc, they had nineteen brigades numbered twenty to twenty nine for construction only. They were all over the island building schools, colleges and hospitals, it was a massive building programme. The officer in charge greeted Alan and he introduced me, taking us inside. He said everything was okay and will be ready for commissioning in three weeks. Ben, Moutan and Cip joined us, and spent a couple of hours looking around, avoiding the white stripes.

'See you later lads, I said,' I'm Going over to Los Vegas, is anyone there?'

They said Sip was there in the mini-van, he was to pick us up around 5:00 am. A half hour ride and we were there in Los Vegas. We came to the exact same looking gates, saw the workers in the same uniforms, an officer greeted us, and took us inside, this was about halfway completed. Cip was there with a soldier by him, he said it was his body-guard. Ronn and John joined us, saying they had to re-fix some machines as they had been fixed straight onto concrete bases, and should have had rubber washers in between to take the vibration, this was important and became useful to us later on.

This site was supposed to have been the first, but problems which were blamed on us and we then blamed on them made us two months behind. Cip said it would be commissioned in six weeks. Ronn and John thought it could be less if Los Banos went well so all the lads would be able to concentrate there.

Alan was pleased but Cip had a frown on his face.

'Right Roy, is there anything you wish to see, if not I would like to introduce you to the Minister of Construction in Havana before he goes home'.

I said okay, and off we went. It was about an hour's run and we were at our destination, Twenty Seven Avenue. All roads in the town were numbered, not named. I believe it was the American way, Fidel had not changed it. Inside, Alan spoke to a lady at the desk who smiled and waved at us to follow. Strange, as this was just an ordinary house like one at home. Opening the door the room was very sparse with a long desk and four chairs. No carpet on the floors, not what you would think of an office for a Minister. But there at the desk was the man who joined me on the plane in Madrid.

'This is Mr. Roy Smith, the new Building Engineer, Mr Lopez' Alan said.

Lopez stood up with a smile and said, 'I believe we have already met, how did you like your flight?'

I was so surprised, words were difficult, and somehow I managed to mutter 'okay' his eyes looked at the ceiling in disbelief, I thought quick Roy, say something to put this right, as he knows I'm not telling the truth.

'But you could have taken the seat at the back and allowed me the front one' I said smiling. His eyes sparkled, and he seemed satisfied that I was being diplomatic. Sitting down, we started to talk to Alan, going over things, ending by Senor Lopez saying he wanted me to concentrate on the other four sites as they were behind with the construction.

'I realise travel will be a problem', said Senor Lopez, 'a vehicle will be arranged to take you to Ciemfago and Matenos you can manage Colon as your mini bus already goes there with the other engineers'. Santiago De Cuba. 'I will have to arrange for tickets to fly there'

After a little chat I left, and returned to our house, Alan telling me that Santiago was the old capital of Cuba and quiet a distance, a two hour flight, and ten hours by road to the other end of the island. That night we all went out for a drink and a meal, my first, and I was surprised how very smart the Yacht Club was, us sitting there like film stars. There were only two drinks available, Carvonor (beer) and Diacara, a rum with ice, with it being very hot I had a Diacara, and being hungry, I began looking for a menu but there was none, after about half an hour the head waiter, immaculately dressed came to the table saying he was very sorry but there was no food available, Cip translated, but apart from me the lads knew as this happened very often in all the restaurants. The thing I was told why they stay open is because everybody has to work whether they do any business or not, and at the end of the week payment is a voucher that entitles you to go to certain warehouses for your food, in other words no voucher, no food, clothes etc.,

'Blimey do we get one' I said.

'Oh yes, Alan gives us all one each, and then we go to the end of the avenue where your warehouse is. We give everything to Ellena and she does her best to feed us.'

To help, we went out every night trying to find a meal. The White House was one, and the other was Dirty Harry's, famous for belonging to Al Capone, these were only for foreigners as you have to pay in hard currency, they would not accept their money (peso's). Sometimes you were lucky to have a meal of chicken, fish, frog's legs or snails.

When the Embassy had their barbecues, which we were invited to, there was always roast pig. That night ended with cheese and hard biscuits. I went to bed ready for the journey to Colan. Cip drove, after one and a half hours we arrived at the same locked gates looking for the workforce, exactly the same construction but not quite finished. This is where I could be of use. Speaking to the officer in charge he said a problem had occurred, two panels were wrong, one space in between was 4.500 mm and the other 3.500, what had happened was that the concrete column was 500mm out of position. Someone had set it out on the wrong side of the mark, but what was the best way to correct it?

By now a number of workers were standing around by us looking very sheepish, the Cubans are a very proud people and were upset that this had happened, one said one panel needed to be out of it, and then welded to the other, yes, but we had welded the panels with massive plastic coated sheets riveted on angle iron straps. We thought about propping up the roof and taking it down and doing a rebuild, yes it would work but it would be a messy job. My solution was to shutter the long side 500mm and concrete it that made 4metres, the panel on the other side cut off the bottom of flange 500mm that would allow it to fit in line and cover the extra width of the concrete pillar. They all looked puzzled and said they would decide later. I spent the rest of the day on the water treatment plant where they were concreting. To my surprise there were about thirty workers mixing with shovels as they had no mixer.

I said 'no it's probably broken down' pointing to a machine that looked like it had not been used for years. In the afternoon a lorry arrived and tipped a load of fruit boxes of bread and other things. The workers all went to it saying it was eating time, pointing to their mouths. God I thought, nothing surprises me now.

Cip came over with a cob of bread filled with something fishy and a very hot sauce with a bottle of water. I thanked him but did not ask where he got them from as this man was a law unto himself.

'Right Roy, its 5:00pm better make tracks' he said.

As we were leaving, the officer came running to us waving and he asked me if he could show me something, it would only take a few minutes, Cip was not very happy, but I went with him to the mistaken columns. There to my surprise it was completed. I looked around and they had taken my advice, the workers were all standing there, eyes fixed on me and with a stern look on their faces.

They must have worked very hard and were exhausted, looking at them I gave a big smile and told them it was 'mucho' very good, excellent. Their faces lit up, and they all wanted to shake my hand even the stripes with their glazed eyes. I thought it was time to go. The officer asked if I was making a report for the minister. 'Yes,' I said 'and it will be good.' He thanked me and Cip roared off.

You have made friends there I thought.

On our way back I was beginning to notice more people living in wooden shacks with a tin sheet roof, very brightly painted and everywhere there were large pictures of Castro and another man.

Cip told me it was Che Guevara, a much loved hero of the Cubans.

Receiving my voucher off Alan, we all went for our rations, one loaf of bread, a packet of butter wrapped in brown paper, a jar of jam (caviar) a one pound bag of sugar, coffee, a tin of Russian pilchards, a packet of plain biscuits (home made), a carton of milk, and one pound of cheese. This was to last for one week.

As a new worker I was allowed one pair of shoes, one pair of jeans and a tee shirt, I told the lady they were not required as I had my own from England and could she give them to a person who needed them.

She gave me an embarrassing hug and I hastily followed the lads up the avenue. We all gave the food to Ellana to perform her miracles for the coming week. I noticed Alan was getting worried and drinking heavily. Youlan told me she knew he was drinking a bottle of Vodka every night.

Monday was the commissioning day or opening day as we called it. Castro was opening it and Alan wanted us all to be there on Sunday making sure everything was ready.

There was an unwritten law in Cuba you work six days for your vouchers, and one day for Cuba.

Arriving at Los Banos, there were hundreds of people cleaning, polishing, brushing, and cleaning the shacks where the prisoners lived. They had all moved to another site. Alan was pleased and we left at lunch time calling at a lovely sandy beach to have a swim.

 Monday morning, and at 6:00am. We were all at Los Banos, getting the machines ready, electricity on, water flowing, and the refrigeration plant was very cold. Cip had left it on all night.

 The animals for the test were chickens, the quantity was 4,000 chickens an hour, from taking out of the gates, hooked up by the legs onto the monorail and coming out the other side frozen, eight hour shifts - thirty two thousand, was there, that many on the island I thought?. At approximately 8:00am Castro arrived, I saw him from the rendering plant, for if there were going to be a problem for me, it would be there. The belt carrying all the waste up into the boiler may have been too steep and sometimes waste would drop off. Alan gave the okay and a man I later knew as Menizes, he was to be the manager of the plant, started pressing the buttons.

Castro and the Ministers were walking along the monorail into the building. Alan looked worried, he probably wanted a drink. Outside the compound there were lots of vehicles, lorries, vans and pick-ups all with chickens. I thought Roy you were wrong, it looks as though they have the numbers, I hope nothing breaks down. At 12:00 am I was told that food and drink were available in the main area, there were chairs for the officials and forms for the rest. I had a piece of pastry and a lovely fruit drink with ice in from Cip's refrigerator. I noticed Castro was very interested in the flakey ice machines. As the flakes came falling down into a container, he kept grabbing a handful.

The machines were all working throughout lunch, at about 3:45 the machines suddenly ground to a halt. Alan had shouted that they had run out of chickens, 30,000 had been slaughtered. It had been a success, thank goodness. Lopez had asked Alan to line us up with the Brigade and all other people who had been part of the project as Castro wanted to thank everyone.

He came along shaking hands and when he came to us, Lopez introduced us as the Hollanders, but when he came to me, Lopez said to him very quietly 'Englishman, just arrived' Castro looked, smiled and shook my hand and said 'Ha, English how you find Cuba?' by this time sweat was pouring out of me and I said instantly 'it's very hot sir' he roared with laughter and touched his head, I took it to be I ought to put a hat on. Later an officer came to me and gave me a Castro cap, one with a large beck just like a baseball cap. I liked to think Castro had sent it. Alan was very pleased, and we all went to The White House and had plenty to drink and had a good frogs legs meal.

Things went well for a few weeks, more time at Los Vegas and that brought things up to schedule. Castro came again, and the process was the same as Los Banos. Alan and the company were very pleased, another load of tobacco, sugar, and coffee were on its way. The barbeques at the embassy being the highlight of the week, there were some very interesting people, sometimes enjoyable, others not so. The Dutch Embassy and Swedes were the best unfortunately the English were the worst.

The ambassador and family, Wynn Jones were rather tongue in cheek with their eight consultants.

I wondered what they all did, as there was only two English on the island, Alan and myself.

The food was embarrassing, a little sausage, cheese and pineapple on a stick and triangle sandwiches of fish paste, but plenty of Chevos, Regal Whiskey and Gordons Gin. I noticed people had difficulty talking to Wynn Jones and family. They had a plum in their mouths. Alistar was one of the consultants that I could converse with. He said that we should have reported to the embassy on arrival as Cuba was a dangerous place for U.K. citizens. I laughed and said they seemed to be alright to me. All the embassy's had joined together in a project that Castro had okayed that was to hire a large warehouse which they all supplied food, clothing and other commodities, the only restriction was only people with a Diplomatic pass could enter and must be paid for in hard currency.

Our rations were not enough, so the Dutch lads all got passes although I always paid my share. I was a little annoyed that myself and Alan were never allowed in, so I told Alan I was going to apply for a pass from the embassy.

'You, want a diplomatic pass?' Wynn Jones said, in his familiar plum voice.

Whatever next, I was ready to give him a mouth full of broken teeth but Alan pushed me away and he said. 'We will have to apply somewhere else.'

Alan wrote to his M.P. in Westminster a Mr. Davies who was secretary to Wilson and Callaghan and within a couple of weeks had a message to go to the embassy to pick up our passes, we had pleasure in putting two fingers up to them.

Things were going very well until Ellena, who was very upset, told me she was leaving. I asked why, she said, Talk to the others.'

I asked and was told some of the boys were bringing prostitutes into the rooms at night, this was dangerous as there was a law that no fraternising was allowed, that's why the army were supposed to patrol the area. The penalty if caught was one year jail for the male and two years for the female. There were already two Swedes in jail so they knew about it being forbidden. I told them they were in trouble because Ellena, Raphael and another translator named Martha were army officers. Alan warned them, and the Dutch embassy people came to talk to them. Lopez had also heard and was worried, but they kept on saying what they did in their private lives was up to them.

By this time twelve weeks was up and I was ready to fly home. Alan asked me to wait a couple of days as they were all going home for Christmas.

I thought yes, we will have a good time flying home together. The day we flew out Raphael and Martha drove the two mini-vans taking us to the airport, when we arrived Raphael took me to one side.

'Senor Roy' as he always called me.

'Be careful, some of the lads are going to be arrested, creep away, stay by Alan, his wife and son'.

Sure enough as we were weighing in at the Liberian airway the army arrived, rifles wavering, they asked for our passports arresting Cip and Ceep and Ben, the girls were already in jail.

Alan asked what the problem was, but got no answer, and he was pushed away. On the plane the other Dutch lads looked very worried. Moutan, I think, knew what was going on because he said there will be trouble at home as they were all married and Cip had two children. I was glad I was going on the Manchester flight from Madrid, Alan was going to report to Head Office which was good until the three lads had been arrested.

I was greeted by my wife at Manchester with our four children, there were lots of hugs and kisses, as I had missed them all.

I had had four wonderful weeks, giving my excuses to Head Office that I was unable to attend the Christmas party, but would meet the others in Cuba. Alan phoned me with Christmas wishes and told me there was hell to pay regarding the lads, their wives had found out, and blamed the company and Alan, the Cuban's had requested three more technicians to replace Ben, Cip and Sip.

I had a better flight returning to Havana on Liberian Airways and was met by Raphael and Alan at the airport. Los Banos had been commissioned. Castro and Lopez were very happy but not willing to release the three lads as there were two Swedes serving the same sentence of one year and they had already served six months.

The new lads Alan had bought with him were two Dutchmen and an Englishman, thank goodness.

At last there was someone I could have a conversation with, his name was John Butterworth, a Biologist engineer for the treatment of the effluent water, he came from Bideford, Devon.

The two Dutch lads seemed okay, Max and Van. Moutan was looking after all the Dutch lads, keeping his eye on them, things were much better now. Moutan became a close friend to me, I accepted him for being in charge and seeing everything was above board as they say.

I noticed Alan was drinking a lot and the lads began calling him the alcoholic. This was getting serious, even Lopez was beginning to use me for reports, this I played down because Alan seemed to be alright with me and so was Moutan. My work was way in front of the other lads on construction, the only time I was on their sites was by request, and when John was having trouble in the water treatment plant.

One morning Martha, a driver and translator in the same position as Raphael, came to John saying there was trouble at Los Vegas and you and Smith were to go there. Off we went, and on arrival saw a number of people on the water treatment plant. Going over and looking down, to our surprise it was full of chickens heads, feet and feathers, all mixed in the waste water. 'Blimey what's happened' said John.

'I think something's gone wrong in the rendering plant let's see. First uncover the last manhole'

It was full of feathers, carrying onto the plant I noticed the conveyor belt was clean and working, the boiler was empty and clean, the floor tidy, but some of the floor grills were off, the men were nervously watching me, but saying nothing. In one corner was a mattress, I guess it was where they had a few hours sleep when things were quiet.

'I know what's happened John' I said. 'The belt was running at top speed instead of medium or slow and when this happens the waste falls off the belt, this is why a man should be here to slow it down or shovel it back onto the belt, but I guess this man fell asleep pointing to the mattress and what he has done is taken the grills off the drains and brushed them down.' What had to be done was to rod the drains and clean out the manholes right up to the treatment plant, to see if we could get some kind of net and fish out the rest in the holding pens.

By now there were quite a number of people around, and Martha carried out my orders to them, they worked all day sweating in the heat, and the smell was horrible, but they did it. Now came a problem making out a report, I told John the man responsible would go to prison or even worse, so could we just say it was a problem that happens from time to time, and they would know what to do when it happens again, and leave it at that. 'Yes' said John. Martha looked puzzled staring at me I just looked at her and said,

'Please, no trouble.'

The weeks went by, about the same time Colon was nearly ready for commissioning. John was still trying to get the water to eighty nine degrees clean but sometimes there was too much chlorine or not enough, and when he got that right the blowers vibrated out of line, this needed attention and adjusting, as John explained to the maintenance man, when you hear it getting louder this is when you adjust it if you don't it will break the belts. Alan came to me to say that I was going to Santiago de Cuba with Lopez, We were flying and staying at one of the best hotels for two nights, and he would give me the money hard currency, to pay for all hotel bills, drink and food for both of us.

'Don't let Lopez pay for anything' he said.

Being at the airport with Lopez was making me feel uncomfortable, as I had not realised how well known and liked he was, people were shaking his hand and some hugging him. I think he felt the same as me.

Lopez found out later he was third in command when Castro and Che Guervara landed with twenty seven men to fight Batista, all the original men had high positions in the government.

As we were walking to the plane I noticed on the tail, faintly painted over, a lady in a chair holding a staff it was the Brittania Airways emblem, this was the first plane my wife, two children and myself flew in, it was called the Whispering Giant, I told Lopez this.

When we boarded the plane I noticed the man sitting next to me was very familiar.

'He's a gold medal runner' said Lopez, it was Quantarina the 'Flying Tiger' who won the 400 metres in the Olympics. I turned, smiled, and offered my hand, which he shook, and speaking in Spanish wanted to know if I was there. Lopez was interpreting for me. 'No I said but I have watched you on television many times, and my C.O. in the army was Roger

Bannister'. 'Oh the four minute miler, a little too far for me.' He said laughing.

'I didn't know you were in the army' said Lopez.

'Yes, two years National Service' I replied.

When we took off, the noise and vibration was horrific, I thought it was to get us airborne but all through the journey it was the same, in fact it got worse. There was little conversation only sign language and to my surprise when we landed everybody clapped and when the pilot came out of the flight deck everybody clapped again. Seeing Lopez he went to him, offering his hand.

'I have flown many times and never witnessed so much applause,' he said. Lopez was greeted at the airport by what I would imagine to be important people, one being a large hipped lady, short dark hair with a miserable looking face, I thought I would not like to cross that lady. After going through all the pandemonium, Lopez came over to me with, of all people the lady in question.

'Smith, this is Claudia Menzies, Chief Building Engineer' he said. Glad to meet you' I said shaking her hand.

'Are you the English engineer who's going to show us where we are going wrong?' she said.

'Oh no from what I've seen the sites are very good' I said, she thanked me and turned away, kissing Lopez, saying she would see him later.

Driving to the Hilton Hotel, the name was again painted over, I thought it must be the same poor paint as The Brittania.

'How did you find Claudia?' he said. 'She's very blunt and personal, she must be very good at her job' I replied.

'She is', said Lopez.

I was taken around the site by a young engineer, there was nothing amiss apart from the water treatment unit that was not positioned at the lowest part of the site. This was always recommended and I thought tomorrow I will investigate it as it was late in the day now.

I didn't know where Lopez was, but at the evening meal he joined me asking how the afternoon had gone.

'Were there any problems?' he asked.

'No things seem to be going well' I said.

'I don't think this will be the last to be commissioned the way things are going, this will be a problem for the other engineers, especially the refrigeration plant, what do you recommend? he asked.

'I think you should bring some of your engineers down here as they are operating the Los Vegas and Los Banos plants, and they should have their understudies ready to carry on alone by now. Lopez Nodded, 'what are you eating?' he said

' Swordfish, I replied, and it's beautiful.'

'I'll have the same' he said to the waiter.

After a good meal, the best I had eaten in all the time I'd been in Cuba, we went to the bar and I had Diacara, Lopez had rum. After breakfast I went with the engineer to the site.

'Claudia was asking me all about the afternoon with you' he said.

'I bet she was' I thought.

Back on site I first investigated the last manhole chamber, it had a larger more powerful pump in to pump the waste to the higher beds, this was okay, no problem, but I could not see why. Next I went over to where the plans show it to be, I knew the plans by heart after being in the drawing office for three months in Amsterdam. After a while I noticed a large mould of rocky land, and this, if they had followed our drawings would be the entrance, yes I thought, they don't have the machines to remove that. I had been talking to some of the prisoners who remembered me from the other sites, one I had remembered well was a man in his thirties, he was slim with receding hair, he was always singing and had a beautiful voice, when I asked someone who he was, I was told he was Frank Sinatra's understudy, and while Frank was away he used to stand in for him especially on the radio. He was well looked after, but he did not look after his own family, hence his twenty year sentence. The young engineer arrived to say I was to go to head office, and see Claudia. Off we went, Claudia met us but there was no hand shake or greeting.

'How do you think the site is going?' she said.

'Very good I said, so far, so good.'

I was puzzled at first why it was different to the other five sites, it had been moved around and I could see why, I would have done the same.

'Yes I had to overcome the rocky mould as the machines are all busy on more important projects' she said.

I noticed her desk was stacked high with drawings of schools, hospitals and universities. 'God, are you in charge of all these?' I said sarcastically,

'Yes' she said smiling. I thought blimey, she's smiled, it's marvellous what a bit of bullshit can do.

I was dropped off at my hotel, had a shower, packed my little holdall and went down to the desk and asked for my bill. Senor Lopez asked what currency I was paying in. I answered Guilders (Dutch), he came back to me with a note saying two rooms, meals and bar tariff was 400 guilders. Alan had given me 500 so I was in pocket. Lopez joined me at the airport thanking me for settling the hotel bill. I said I was instructed by Alan to do so. 'Smith, I would like to see you in my office one day, I'll inform you when and thank you, you've made a good impression on a lot of people.' He said.

The flight back was just the same, what an experience but I was used to being surprised by now.

I left with Raphael, he drove me home and I noticed he was very quiet, I asked him if he was okay, 'problems Senor, but Moutan will tell you.' he said

Entering the house everybody was sitting around with glum faces. 'What's the matter?' I said.

'Alan's gone home with his wife and son as the baby is unwell.' Moutan said.

'Well that's no problem as long as they are alright, we will carry on as before.' I said.

The men seemed to be more at ease, and they decided to go out for a meal, as they were going out John gave me a letter from Yola, Alan's wife. On the front of the envelope was written *To Roy*. I opened it and it said that Alan was very ill, but they had said it was the baby so they could fly out immediately, they would be more understanding at the airport as its very difficult without the exit visas. Raphael had a letter for Lopez saying the same.

The next day Raphael was to take me to the office, the other lads went with Martha to the sites. 'Roy I suppose you know what's happened to Alan and family?' he said.

'Yes' I said. 'Well He's left you in charge and we agreed, what do you say?'

'I don't think this will go down very well with the Dutch lads or Amsterdam, I would recommend us carrying on as before, Moutan looking after the Dutch, with me in front looking after construction, and Butterworth on the treatment plant' I said.

'But who will report to me and carry out my requests?' he said.

'I think I can do that but let me have a word with Moutan I'm sure he will agree.

'Okay but I would like to see you to-morrow at 2.00 pm. It's very important you are there.' he said.

That night I spoke to Moutan, I told him the position and asked if he would agree between ourselves any requests from Lopez to be passed on to me.

'Yes, I've never told anyone, but one day John mentioned some of the lads objected to Moutan 'checking on them' he said. 'Well Moutan is really in charge he's been here the longest,

'Ah' I said. But Moutan is a Malucan only half Dutch, and I think racism is creeping in. 'Bloody hell John haven't we got enough problems without this.'

So for the next few days I was watching Moutan's back, if there was any back chat, I pulled them up straight away, making it clear I was backing Moutan. The meeting at 2.00 pm at 27th street was very worrying for me as Castro was there just sitting around the table smoking a cigar with the other officers, some in uniforms. Lopez began the meeting by saying. 'Smith, we were wondering if you are able to help us as we know you have a diplomatic pass, much to the annoyance of your Embassy, so you have some influence.

'Bloody hell' I thought, I'm only a hairy arsed bricklayer.

'I'm sure you have noticed that our planes will not last very long, continued Lopez, we are desperate for spares, if you remember meeting me in Madrid, that is what I was trying to order but had no help, the planes were all bought from', looking at Castro, who read out, British Airways, Basingstoke, Hampshire in a peculiar Spanish accent.

'Have you also noticed that our public transport is becoming smaller, as one bus breaks down it is cannibalised to repair others, we need spares for them also, as we thought of looking to Castro again', who said 'British Leyland, Lancastershire' in his broken Spanish. 'We are willing to trade, but as you know the sanctions put on our people are making it very difficult, a lot of countries are helping us you know, for instance The Hollanders. I will do my best' he said, looking at Castro again, but I'm not as important like you are sir'

'Bullshit' I thought, I could be in a lot of trouble, the responsibility on my shoulders was getting pretty heavy. They all thanked me and asked me to leave as they had a lot of business to discuss.

Going to all the Embassy's parties and barbecues, I tried to ask for help in getting the spares but every time I mentioned British the answer was the same, no chance, it was well known Cuba had bought the planes and buses from the U.K. before sanctions came into force, they agreed it was wrong but U.K. was a puppet of U.S.A. which I did not like but held my tongue. I was waiting for the British Embassy party, feeling that I was going to say a few things that people were thinking but not saying. When the time came I was ready, John felt the same, we were going to have words. Why can't we help these people for spares? I asked the ambassador forcefully, which startled him. The reply was 'because they have men fighting in Angola and they should not fight in other people's wars.

'You must be joking aren't you?' I said. 'I've been in our army, we fought in Korea, Malaysia, Cypress, Aden and now in Northern Ireland and you disagree on 500 soldiers fighting in Angola, is it worth all the suffering these people are going through.

'Hear, hear' shouted John.

'I must ask you to leave' said the Consulate, he could see the Ambassador and his family were getting upset so we were kicked out. To be fair, a number of other people left too. I was told later everyone had left by 9.00 pm. Which was unusual as this usually went on until the early hours of the morning.

Weeks later I was told they had been recalled to the U.K. after poor reports from other Embassy's. Before leaving Cuba I was going down with Dengue, a tropical fever, although I had taken my malaria tablet each morning, this was a kind of malaria that had I not taken them then I would have caught the full blown infection which is similar to our flu, I was three days in bed taking aspirins. John also had it but became worse, so we took him to the Diplomat hospital, saying he was Dutch. He was in for a week in an oxygen tent I think we caught it from the mosquito's in the water treatment plant, that is where they bred.

The lad's had booked a table at The Cocobanor Night Club, hoping to cheer me and John up after our illness. It was a most enjoyable evening the show was out of this world, beautiful girls coming down from the trees singing, and Carmen Miranda with her hat full of fruit. Castro was there, all smiles, and looking at us from time to time. I think he wanted us to show him that we were enjoying ourselves, because Lopez asked if we had enjoyed the show.

On our way to Cienfagos I stopped, as I had seen some people who I had seen at the Embassy. They asked what I was doing here. They were building a clinic for Lepers, I was surprised, I didn't know there were Lepers in Cuba.

'Yes' they said. 'A lot of Caribbean islands have a few, but only mild cases as they are being treated now.

Would you like to see them?' they said, 'Yes' I replied, and I followed them through a tobacco plantation. There on the other side were a few huts, one with half a roof on. The people had some sort of disfiguration but not as bad as I have seen on films and television.

'We are short of timber, tin sheets and nails' they said.

'I am at the slaughter plant about a mile away, if you call I will see what I can do' I said.

What's that place? I asked, it was a large concrete area like an aircraft runway with long round tubes about 60 feet long. 'Don't ask', they said, 'but where there's a leper clinic you will see one of those, it is supposed to keep people away, as you already know, prisons are building sites, but there is one that's along the coast line about ten miles from Havana, half under the sea, it is where foreigners are taken', I know that two Swiss lads, three Dutch lads and seven Americans from the Bay of Pigs were on an attachment that went wrong, it was supposed to have been instigated by the Americans, these eleven Americans were supposed to have been there' I said.

'How do you know?' I was asked.

'Because I've been there, and there are only seven.' I replied.

Alistar looked at me waiting for some more information but I thought, that's enough Roy, he'll get you into trouble, the embassies never helped John and so I thought 'sod you mate'.

I'd never seen a hurricane before, only on film, it's a horrific sight, the wind and waves about sixty feet high, were pounding the promenade and road along the front of Havana, ripping the roads up and slamming into the other side, hitting the building such as the hotel I had stopped in for a drink. The building was shaking as though it was in an earthquake, up to 1000 people lost their lives so I was told. They called it 'Hurricane Hugo', the damage it did set the Cubans back years, but not one western country came to their aid. I never looked on the Caribbean Sea the same again. When I see the beautiful, calm sea, clear as tap water with all kinds of colourful fish, I think 'yes' I've seen you when you've been angry ,taking people's lives, showing no mercy at all.

This reminds me of the time I joined Moutan, he was a scuba diver, borrowing the air tanks from the Dutch Embassy. We went to the Valderama beach, as Ben said that the coral reef was full of life. We never spent more than twenty minutes at a time under water. After Moutan had finished, he fixed me up, and I being a good swimmer, he started me with mollusk, which are a delicate shell that are found in the area.

As he ran out of air, he gave the thumbs up to me and left, pointing to my watch which meant I had twenty minutes left. I kept to the coral reef, looking for conch, another elaborate shell found in the area which was what I was diving for. I would have liked a large one and I thought with the air tanks

I could swim further down than the locals, and sure enough I found a beauty.

As I was cleaning it I felt my hairs on the back of my head raise, it's funny, but we all have a sense of danger, and I felt this when looking down searching. Danger was there, four or five sharks about twelve feet long, circling below me, gliding so beautifully as though they had not seen me. Then I caught sight of a silver shape over my shoulder gliding over me about six feet away, then about four feet away was another shark with a black eye like a bead, swimming one way then another. I had frozen by this time. I had the sense to keep as close to the reef as possible but not enough to cut myself as the coral was sharp.

 My legs felt paralysed, I could not move them, my knees were shaking out of control. I had felt this sensation before when I was boxing in the army, I thought *this is shock*. The sharks kept on coming towards me trying to knock me away from the coral, as if they were afraid of cutting themselves. Little by little I inched my way along the coral, my watch told me another five minutes and my time would be up. I thought I have got to swim along the edge of the coral as Moutan would be keeping his eye on the time. This bloody shark kept brushing me closer and closer, but the others never came up to look, they must have been quite a distance away, it's difficult to measure that they were still there. Inch by inch I made my way, dragging my legs as I had no feelings, till at last I looked up and saw the sunlight shining down, I thought it can't be far now.

Then there was a loud bang, the shark dived down by my side and it had gone, then I saw Moutan with a machete, banging on the coral, he had seen the shark and had frightened it away. Moutan dragged me up onto the sandy beach, with an anxious look on his face,

'Are you alright?' he said.

'No, I replied, my legs are frozen and my knees are knocking can you rub them for me? this has happened to me before, they will be alright in a few minutes.' I said.

'I have been coming here for about twelve months and have never seen a shark here before, it's a good job you had the sense to keep close to the reef.' he said.

'And I kept hold of my Conch, I was going to hit the shark with it' I joked.

We both laughed, I never did any more diving again and I don't think Moutan did.

I was going along the sea front in Havana watching people cleaning up the mess Hugo had made, there arrived a couple of lorries with men inside, I was told they were going to

Miami as the Americans had said Castro would not allow Cubans to leave, so he was sending 50 men who wanted to go but neglected to say they were all convicted homosexuals.

John got me into trouble with the Germans at the embassy party. A couple of Germans, who had had a few drinks too many, started to take the piss out of us 'Hollanders' as they called us, saying we were taking all this time to open one factory. They had heard we were better workers in bed.

John got angry, and before I could stop him he had told them some of us were British and said

'We have beaten you twice, how many more times do you want a beating?'

We were asked politely to leave.

'Kicked out again Smithy?' said Alistar, who was outside the Embassy.

He then introduced me to someone called Mark, who was a man in his fifties.

'He is the third Englishman on the island, and has lived here before the revolution for a company called Tate and Lyle, they ran the sugar plantations, Mark was the only one that didn't run, so he was made manager and lived in George Raft's old house.'

'I've seen a lot of films with him in, what's it like? I said.

Mark told me it was not as glamorous as you might think as all these beautiful houses were ransacked after the Revolution, and everything that could be moved was stolen and the only thing left in his place was the beautiful staircase which was 10 feet wide in the centre of the vast hall and at the top was divided to the left and right just like on the films. He went on to tell me that every mansion was the same, it must have had the same contractor.

'You can see where Frank Sinatra lived, his is the one with the grand piano shaped swimming pool.' Mark said.

'Yes, I've seen that, the Ambassador lives there' I replied.

Mark said that Al Capone's house was turned into Council Offices in one half and Public Toilets the other. 'It's true' Mark said laughing.

'One of your chaps is always playing my favourite music in that mini V.W. bus.'

'That's me' I said. I have Neil Diamond tapes, all his songs, would you like to borrow them?'

'Yes' he said.

'But better still I'd like to buy them they are like gold dust here.'

'When I go on my break to the U.K. you can have them, I will buy new ones to bring back.' I said.

Martha was waiting outside to take us home.

'In trouble again Butterworth?' she said.

'Yes darling' he said kissing her on the forehead.

Martha and Raphael missed nothing as I later found out, there were times when soldiers would salute them or clip their heels so this told me they were officers, I preferred them to drive because the Dutch lads caused trouble in Cuba because of the shortage of public transport, it was against the law to drive past people waiting for a bus if you had a seat empty in your vehicle. Sometimes the police (army) would stop us pointing to the empty seat

'Capitalist' The Dutch lads would shout, and no one would enter the van, where the police would kick the sliding door shut. This I found embarrassing and where ever possible told Martha and Raphael they must stop if they have empty seats which was much to the annoyance of some of the Dutch lads. They lall looked very sheepish, no acknowledgement or handshake. Time was racing very fast, work was good and soon my twelve weeks were up. I was really looking forward to seeing my wife and children. Meeting Joyce at Manchester was wonderful, but she began to cry, I asked what the problem was and she said I had lost a lot of weight. I didn't realise but I had lost 2 stone in 13 weeks. I enjoyed my four weeks leave and I started to regain my weight. Later I received a phone call from Yola saying Alan was in re-hab and did I know he had been sacked.

'No' I said.

'I've heard nothing but I'll find out and let you know.'

A few days later I received a letter asking me to come to a meeting at Head Office on the 12th April, all the technicians had been requested to attend and no way was I to go to Cuba before this. This suited me, a few days more at home.

The day arrived, everyone was there at Head Office, John and Moutan came towards me saying,

'The bastards have got Alan the sack because of his drinking.'

'Yes I know is there anything we can do?' I said.

'No there are too many against us'.

The meeting was called to order, all of us sitting around a large table. Rikham, the head of Alfa Engineering who I worked for, began to speak.

The meeting was called by five other companies who had technicians in Cuba, although Alfa was the main contractor, we were all members of the Stock Duke group, and the other companies had requested Alan Walsh to be dismissed due to his alcoholic addiction and for not controlling the situation correctly regarding the three technicians that were in prison. We, meaning Alfa, Rikham said had done this, but another complaint made by the five was the appointment of Mr. Roy Smith an Englishman being in charge of a Dutch project. It should be a Dutchman and not to be dictated to us by Cuban Authorities.

After Rikham had spoke, the others in turn had their say, but they spoke in Dutch so I could not comment, but I guessed they didn't like the English or the Cubans, this went on for hours.

After which they said we would have lunch and resume at 2.00 pm. That gave me a chance to think of what to say when it came to my turn. I asked John his opinion.

'Tell them to get stuffed, he said, it wasn't Alan's fault or yours that they were frigging about with prostitutes, they were spineless, make them say what's on *their* minds not their bosses.'

'Right Mouton, what about you? I asked, I would like to speak after you because I would like to back you up this time no matter what you say.'

We had a good lunch and conversation with Demag then we all took our seats. Rikham started by asking if I would I like to say anything?

'Yes' I said.

'But first I would like the five lads to tell me what I've done wrong.'

'Right, we will go round and ask them,' not one said a word, the manager had said it all was the answer.

'What's wrong with being English? have you forgotten my father and my relations got the Germans out of your country?' I said.

'When they walked, let me say again walked in, I continued. Their faces were a picture to behold, they were stunned. Your three technicians are in prison because they were not properly interviewed by yourselves' I said.

'picking men who were more interested in picking up prostitutes then doing their work, since they have been away the projects have come on in leaps and bounds, making up for lost time, the Cubans are very pleased, trade is moving more quickly so Head Office surely has seen the difference.' I went on.

They began talking in Dutch, shouting at Rikham, when Moutan stood up and in a loud voice gave a speech spoken in Dutch for about five minutes. I don't know what he said, but it seemed to quieten everyone down and they looked rather sheepish. I thought Rikham had asked all the technicians to leave the room as he wanted to talk to the Companies. We went into an adjoining room John telling the other five to piss off, or they would have their F----- faces smashed. They disappeared.

After about one hour the door opened and they came out. Demag told me they had been outvoted and the Cuban project was stopped forthwith. We would all be offered other contracts. Demag said Rikham wanted a word, so I went into the other room where he and Mr. Prins were talking. Seeing me he said.

 'Sorry Roy but my hands are tied, and we are not big enough to carry the load ourselves we don't want to lose you, we will pay your salary, don't worry about your money, but we would like you to accept another contract in Libya to finish

your present contract and see how you like it. If favourable
we would like to offer another contract, we all think a lot
about you, though your speech was very hurtful, we are not
all like that you know, my father was killed in the war.'

'Sorry' I said.

'I would like to think things over with my wife, thank you.' I
said.

We shook hands then I made my way to the airport and
home.

Libya

After the Cuba contract was cancelled I was seconded to the German Company Empro for three months to finish my contract. They offered me a position of Site Engineer Manager in Libya with a ten per cent raise in salary, so my life with the Arabs, Sahara Dessert and Colonel Gaddafi began.

The plane from Manchester to Tripoli was Caledonian Airways, it was an excellent flight with good food and plenty of drinks which everyone took advantage of as in Libya there was no alcohol.

I was met by Brian Lloyd, the manager who greeted me and introduced me to Hussein Soufraki, who was very smartly dressed in western clothes but could not help to be recognised as an Arab.

There were three more engineers on the flight, one was married with two children.

'Do you know them?' asked Ben.

'No' I answered.

Brian rounded them all up, and introduced us, and we were through Tripoli to the office.

They interviewed us one at a time, the guy with his family were going to Sirte, a site about half an hour drive away and they would be staying at a Hotel in the city. I did not see them again but was told they lasted for just two weeks and went back home. The second guy was going to Misrata was an interpreter as he spoke good Arabic, he lasted two months. The third guy with long shoulder length hair was told he was not suitable as he had refused to have his hair cut. He went back on the same plane he arrived on. Of course I did not know about this until later, which was probably as well as I might have joined him on the plane back home.

It was my turn to be interviewed and Brian told me that because I was older, I would be going to Watia, an Airfield construction site which was being constructed by the Italian personnel, it was six months behind schedule. I was to be regarded as a Consultant to find out why, and to help if possible. All this time Sourfraki never took his eyes off me. I had been used to this eye balling by better men than you I thought. It must have done the trick as he nodded to Brian and left the room not saying kiss my --- or anything. I didn't see him again for over three months.

Brian invited me to say with him and his family for the night and he would take me to Watia in the morning, it was about four hours drive in the desert. Christine, his wife a blonde haired young lady around twenty eight years old I would have thought, with a four year old son named Robert.

I was up about 6:00 am the next morning for coffee and toast, with Brian Christine and Robert still in bed.

We started our journey in a Peuguot 407, Brian was a very fast driver, taking the coast road toward Tunisia, Brian was doing most of the talking, describing places as we went through them. One place of interest was Sabbatha a roman town with the ruins of buildings and a lovely beach. This was the nearest place to the sea and the lads used it a lot. We were heading for a town called Azura on the Tunisian border as we turned left onto a beautiful tarmacced straight road.

'It's like this for about 200 miles' Brian said. We were motoring at 100 miles per hour.

'I consider myself as an Office Manager, you guys are what I call Outside Managers as I have no qualifications in your field, my family are a cricketing family in Lancashire.' he said.

'Oh yes, opening bat.' I said.

'That's my cousin, I don't play but my brother does, what's your background are they construction people?' he said.

'Oh no I'm the only one in the building trade apart from my brother who's a Plumber, our background is sailing until they came to the Potteries to work in the Steel industry. Some of the Smiths went back to sailing, which was never mentioned after a certain ship went down.' I said.

'Bloody Hell' said Brian.

'I was feeling myself nodding off.

'Are you alright? This is very monotonous driving, we are nearly there, it's a good job this is an army road else we would never get there, there's nothing but sand as you can see.' he said.

In the distance I could see the road was blocked and as we arrived two soldiers came out of the hut at the side, it looked as though they had been asleep. They looked at Brian's papers then lifted up the barrier. About a mile on the left hand side I could see what looked like caravans, Brian turned and drove right up to them stopping at one. Out came a small rather plump dark haired fellow. Brian greeted him saying 'Zella how are you?' 'Very well thank you' he said with an Italian accent.

'Roy this is Zella, the engineer in charge' Brian said.

'How do you do' I said, shaking hands. By now a lot of other men gathered around us, 'the men are coming in from the site at this time as it is too hot, we start again at 3pm.' said Zella.

'Please join us in the canteen for lunch' he said.

We did just that, we had rice with a spicy stew, very nice drinks of all flavours and cannalone for dessert,' this is alright' I thought.

'Have you Mr. Smith's accommodation sorted out' said Brian.

'Yes, he's in my trailer' said Zella.

The trailers were about 30 feet long with two bedrooms one at each end with a bathroom/toilet in the middle, electricity and water was attached, I thought it was very good. While I was unpacking my cases Brian was talking and discussing things with Zella and the men, he had letters and money which he gave to them. Coming back to me he said. 'Do you think you'll be alright?'

'Yes' I nodded,

'You are to share the Fiat with Zella on the camp, but if you go out take Halima with you, he is your bodyguard, driver and interpreter, I'm going to see the camp Colonel Juma, if I have time I'll call back but if not, you are welcome to my house, you know where I live, if I am not in the office, at week-ends somebody is always going into Tripoli so transport is no problem.'

 Shaking hands, I drove off in the direction of some other building I later found out to be the Camp Headquarters. There were forty Italian workers plus Zella and now myself, also two Turks, Halima was one of these and the other was Said. There were two Pakistan's, Joseph and Zahoor, one Somalian electrical engineer and one African helping in the cookhouse named Jamba, there were forty eight in total.

In all, there were sixteen trailers, plus one canteen, one laundry, one cookhouse, one storeroom, an office and a trailer for recreation. The water was connected to the main supply pipe going to the army camp. We had our two electric generators one as a stand-by. Zella was very friendly and nothing was any trouble for him when I asked for information, but I noticed for some unknown reason the men did not have much respect for him. It did not take me long to see the problem as to why the programme was behind.

Of the forty men, only twelve, plus two Turks and two Pakistani's were working on the site, others were working in the camp, and four plus Jamba in the cookhouse, an eight hour shift and then being taken off by another four plus poor old Jamba doing another eight hour shift totalling 5:am to 10:pm with a one hour break in between.

Hours of work were 6:30am start until the 11:30am siesta, then starting again at 3:30pm until 7:30pm totalling nine hours. There was no Saturday or Sunday work except for the cooks. There was also four men cleaning trailers, four men in the Laundry , four men looking after the generators plus all the plant, for example the machines, as they had to be under cover due to the heat. They used to get very hot, you could not touch them never mind drive them. This had been going on for over twelve months and they wondered why the contract was six months behind.

Our contract was to install rainwater drain pipes all around the runways and taxi ways, collecting any rainwater and transporting it into the large containers which held around a thousand gallons, with top pumps connected to hoses and jets in case of accidents or fire. On the airfield were two squadrons, one French Mirage and one Russian Mig, so you could see how important it was to have water in emergencies, as these machines cost millions of dollars.

Also around the outside perimeter, which was five miles long was another drain to collect rainwater off the road that went all around the perimeter, and that was pumped into the containers. Alongside was another drain to collect all the sewerage water and was pumped to a treatment plant. This was very interesting, as after treatment the water was filtered along troughs into the desert and the men had grown beautiful melons, tomatoes, potatoes and all sorts of vegetables and fruit. At first I did not fancy eating anything from there, the men said the same, but after a while they had started to eat everything.

Because of the distance, levels could not give the falls or the pipes in place would be above ground and that would not be possible unless they invented sky hooks. They had built chambers and put a pump in to pump up to another level and then carry on again. One day as I was driving around I noticed the men standing around so I stopped and asked what the matter was. 'Have you a problem?' I asked. 'Yes' said Zahoor in English, 'we are waiting for Zella to give us the level of the drain, these drains are six metres long and must have the necessary fall.'

'How many pipes do you do a day' I asked.

'Two' he said.

'How many could you do if you had levels?'

'Four or maybe six' he said.

'I'll have a word with Zella' I replied.

That night at the evening meal I told Zella I would like to put the levels in for Zahoor's gang to help him out while he carried on with other things.

'By all means if you want to' he said, 'no problem, I'd welcome the help.'

Next day I told Zella I required two men from the camp with a hammer, saw and nails and white paint if possible, I was going to put levels all along the runway and road. Gathering the Dumpy level and tripod, with the staff I set off with the other men. Much later two men arrived who looked rather miserable, saying in Italian that they were laundry men, and they did not know how to do this job. Zahoor who translated for me was standing by the timber pegs. I told him to saw the timbers in three foot lengths and show these fellows how to do it. I knew that being shown what to do by Zahoor belittled them and they soon got the hang of it. By 11:30am we had put over a mile of levels in. Those I am sure those who've seen many times stakes with a strap on top painted white, the pipe layer holds is called a trammel. When the top was level with the top of the levels on the road that is ready to place in the pipe. If it was higher he told Zahoor to take out some more ground if he took too much it would show the top of the trammel lower, therefore Zahoor had to put some back. After a while, we got used to this system, it was very rare that you had to replace material back. Also they had already laid two pipes each six metres long.

'How are you going on Roy?' Zella asked.

'Okay, this afternoon I'm going on the runway to put the same levels in for Joseph's gang' I said.

'You must go to the control tower first' said Zella and ask permission as they may be flying, sometimes they say no, other times it's okay, and sometimes they ask you to work in another area'.

This time I got the ok, but the following day we could not start until the afternoon. Some of the officers were learning to fly, and it became very dangerous at times, how true this was after seeing some of them, the problem seemed to be in landing, sometimes with a bump, other times going off the runway and others going through the perimeter fence and smashing on to the road. That day Zahoor had laid four pipes which were twenty four metres, Josef had laid three pipes eighteen meters, so myself and the two laundry men had more or less doubled the work. Zella was very pleased.

'I did not have the time to do this' he said rather sadly 'I had Smiley the Secret Service Officer, here all morning, he wanted to know all about you, he hopes you don't drink Scotch and have a camera.'

'No I've been warned about those things' I said.

I told the men I wanted to work at the week-end, and were there any men who wanted extra money. They would be paid in Dinars, I could not get hard currency but another week-end you would have dinars and would not spend your own hard currency in Tripoli or Sabbatha. Sixteen people put their names forward and so we worked through until the next week-end that we had off. I was shattered, it was not the work it was the heat. Some mid-day's it got to one hundred and twenty degrees and that was too hot to work. Brian had given me one thousand dinars to spend, so I was able to pay the men and off we went to Tripoli. My first call was to the office. There were no international phone calls allowed, you had to go to the main Post Office and queue for a kiosk, this took about two hours and after I waited I was able to speak to Joyce and the kids, she said everything was fine, she had not received any of my letters, and I had not received hers, but it was the first time in the office, so I may have had the letters there. I told her I would phone again the following week.

Back in the office Brian was there talking to Zella, seeing me he handed me an airmail.

'I've just been speaking to my wife about this, thanks' I said.

Brian didn't say anymore, he gave me time to read my letter.

He was pleased at the progress made, the drawings in his office showed that. While I was there I noticed a funnily dressed man going up stairs. I asked Brian about him.

'Oh he's your friend from Holland, the Dutch Embassy is above' he said.

I thought its Mr. Prins,

'Can I go up Brian' I asked. 'Yes, he said no problem, I'm sure they will welcome you.'

so upstairs I went, and going through the door I saw Prins, his face lit up.

'Smith how are you doing?' he said, hugging me.

'I'm 'okay, I said, what are you doing here?

'We have a factory to build at Sirte, are any of the lads there?' he said.

'No' I said, 'the three lads are still in prison, we cannot get them out.

He asked how I was getting on.

I said I was okay.

'Ah good, only it was myself who recommended you to Brian, it won't be long before your contract is up and we hope you will take this factory on for us.' he said.

'I don't think so' I thought. After chatting about old times I went back down to Brian, he wanted me to stay overnight at his place, as he had been invited by the embassy to a meeting in the square, Gaddafi was speaking and would I join him.

'We have to show our faces' he said.

That night we joined people from the embassy sitting near the front, the rest of the people were standing. There must have been thousands there, and as soon as Gaddafi arrived everybody cheered and clapped, even we got up and clapped politely. He must have spoken for over an hour and I never understood a word, but carefully weighed him up, he was slim, not as tall as I had thought and was dressed in white robes, he must have a make-up artist for his face looked as though he had thick make-up on, his eyes were like sharks, round, black, like two beads, no white around them. Every now and then the crowd cheered and clapped, 'what a load of rubbish' I thought, but said nothing.

When Gaddafi had finished he walked along nodding and acknowledging us.

'Thank god that's over Brian' I said. 'I'm tired and hungry, 'we'll pick up a chicken and salad on our way home' I said.

Next morning Halima picked me up. I said farewell to Brian and his family and started for Watia.

That night I had a meal with Zella who had wondered where I was.

'Tomorrow we shall carry on as before' he said. So I retired to my trailer.

Day after day it was the same, nothing out of the ordinary except I was beginning to find out more about the men, for instance Zahoor who was the 'Himac' digger driver (J.C.B.) he was also an interpreter, he could speak six languages and yet had never attended any school,

'How come?' I asked.

'By working with them for years,' he replied. Josef the other Pakistani digger/driver was a surveyor.

'How is it you are not putting these levels in?' I said.

'Zella never asked me' he replied.

'Jamba, who cleaned the kitchen was a chef but Zella preferred an Italian to do the cooking. Soloman, the electrician was okay but I did not like him testing the wires in the trailers, if he jumped when he touched them he would say. 'That's live'.

'Soloman, I said, I'll get you an instrument that will tell whether it's live or not, so don't do that anymore.'

'No problem Mr. Roy' he said smiling.

Bloody hell I thought, it's a good job it's only 110 volts, never the less, I will not be touching them.

Halima was the lorry driver bringing the pipes from a depot to wherever the men wanted them. He also had a large tank that he would lift on to the lorry to fetch diesel, Naffton, as they called it. Also he would get up very early to drive two hours there and two hours back each morning with new bread. Said was the driver of the Cat with a large bucket in front, he loaded the pipes onto the lorry and he would lift them off. Wherever Halima went Said followed, they had been told to look after me so they regarded themselves as my bodyguards.

 'Who told you that' I asked. 'Hussein Sourfraki' said Halima. Said later told me Halima was Hussein's brother in law, he had married his sister.

We worked one weekend if the men wanted the extra money and went to Tripoli the next to make phone calls, and on our way back we stopped at Sabbatha to see the roman ruins and to have a swim, but we had to be in the airfield premises before dark, this was a problem as it went dark very quickly at 8:00pm. The guards would stop us from going to our camp, inside we would have to sleep in our vehicles until sunrise. This I was going to stop one way or another.

It was a four hour drive to Tripoli, and four hours to get back, it didn't leave much time to do any shopping or sightseeing, especially if you had waited two hours to make a phone call.

I was told that here was meeting in the officers mess the next day at 2:00pm and Colonel Juma had asked that I attend.

'What's all that about?' I asked.

'We have one of these meetings every now and again' I was told.

Next morning there seemed more movement than usual. Sometimes you could be working all day and not see anything or any vehicles, but today they were going past all the time.

'Something is going on Mr. Roy.' said Zahoor

At 12:00 pm everybody made their way to camp for lunch and then siesta. Zella looked smart, ready for the meeting. I thought I'd better do the same. At 1:30 Zella said we would take Halima with us he can drive, also the Arab guards don't bother him. We drove up to the army headquarters and the guards stopped us, but I spoke a few words and they let us in, there was no trouble. Zella guided us into a large room which I took to be their recreation room or library as there were a lot of books on the shelves. At the far end was a stage with about six empty chairs, men were sitting all around the room, and to my surprise also there were Brian and Sourfraki with another man who I later knew as Marchello, Zella's Italian boss. I had seen quite a few of these men but had never spoken to them. Following Zella, we managed to find a couple of seats. I would say that there were about twenty men in the room. After a few minutes someone shouted, and in came Colonel Juma and to my surprise Gaddafi, followed by four officers. We all stood and clapped as they sat down. Juma addressed us by saying the project was behind schedule and our leader wished to know what can be done to bring it forward.

'Can you tell us of any constructive ideas', he said, 'it would be appreciated and to please speak the International language.'

The first man to speak was a Russian pilot instructor who was behind in night flights because of no lights on the runways. Mr. Ram was an Egyptian electrician in charge of all the lights and control towers on the runway, and he spoke saying the duct pipes which the electric cables travel through had not been laid yet. Mr. Lee, the Korean engineer was behind because he had no electricity supply yet, and was only coping with portable generators. He was responsible for a large hanger that held the helicopters and spares being constructed by his Korean workforce. Hans, a German engineer was the only one who was on schedule constructing concrete hangers to house the Migs and Mirages. Marchello then spoke, saying he had problems with the workforce and the exceptional heat. There had been no rain in Watia for four years, and it was on his men's shoulders that delivery of materials was late, but we now had them on site and there were extra men and engineers to bring us back up to schedule. Permission given to work week-ends by Colonial Juma was a big help. 'What a load of rubbish,' I thought I had never seen this man before. Sourfraki was as bad, I only saw him two months ago when I arrived in Tripoli. After a lot more discussing, the meeting finished with Gaddafi telling us we must push forward as with the unsettling world today he must have these airfields operationally. They left through the same door they entered with Juma coming back to speak to Sourfraki and then they went together in the other room. Brian and Marchello came over to me and Zella introduced me.

The Italians started to speak in their native tongue, so Brian and I moved away, we knew Sourfraki' was in trouble, but the Arabs would not let us see them quarrelling.

'Why' I said, it's not his fault the Italians are not very good workers.' 'Yes he is the main contractor apart from the Russian instructor all these work for us' said Brian. 'Bloody hell,' I thought, I didn't know that the German came across with Mr. Lee the Korean.

Brian introduced me to them. Hans Winderhoff, the German, said he had seen me on the side of the road putting in levels, 'it looks as though you are motoring at last, is there anything I can do to help?'

'It looks as though we need a lot of help' I said.

The Russians were very friendly, everybody was, except the French instructors who were teaching the Liberians to fly the Mirages. I didn't know what their problem was but they didn't like us at all.

'They don't like anybody so don't worry' said Hans. 'I'm to supply you with concrete, but have not had any requests and I notice all your manholes are filling up again with the sand. You'll have a problem cleaning them out again.'

'Thanks, I'll look into that.' I said.

Mr. Lee said he was very sorry but my men were waiting, 'perhaps we can help your men to put the pipes in, I have no machines but a lot of men.'

'Thanks.' I said. I'll let you know.

'Brian, there's no excuse for being behind, the help is here, Zella has only to ask by the sounds of it' I said.

'I seem to be getting too involved, I said,' I have only another four weeks to go and I'm off home.'

'Christ Roy, I was hoping you would accept a contract from me to carry on, name your own contract I think Sourfraki will except it.' he said.

Brian came into camp late at night saying could we fix him up for the night as they were staying and would be going back to-morrow. Sourfraki was staying with Juma.

'Yes, you can have the spare bed in my trailer.' I said.

Later that night when Zella went to his own room Brian told me that the Italians were going to be sacked, and I was to recruit another contractor to finish the work.

'What's your advice?' he asked.

'You know my position so it's not for me to say.'

'Well' I said.

'Well what would you do? I'll be very grateful of any help I'm only Office Manager not an engineer like you.' he said.

'Well, Zella is a brilliant organiser in the camp, the trailers and food are excellent, the camp is spotless, but outside he's useless. He's got more men inside the camp than on the site this upset some of the men putting the pipes in while the others are in camp living the life of Riley.' I said.

'Well, in the morning I'm going to tell Zella you are to take control of outside, he is to help you with anything you want, and let's see if that improves in the last four weeks you have, I'll put Sourfraki off until the end of your contract and then I hope I've convinced you to stay'. he said.

'No chance' I thought.

The last few weeks saw a big improvement, only one incident worth mentioning was Hans inviting me to his place near Tripoli for the week-end. This was a two bedroom bungalow type of dwelling in what was called a holiday village on the coast. When we arrived there was a message for Hans saying that there was a barbeque at number eight, and he was invited.

'Good, no cooking' said Hans' and there's always plenty to eat and drink at these do's.'

We had a walk down to number eight, it was full of Africans in colourful dress and, guess who's barbeque it was, President Idi Amin's, and his many wives.

'Bloody Hell Hans' I gasped. The world is looking for this man after he fled from Uganda, and here he is with us, I wonder if I dare ask him if he remembers me?'

There were a few German friends of Han's , a few Italians, the rest were Libyans, about thirty people in all and yes, the food was good, chicken, pork, salad and desserts, it was very enjoyable. Han's friends introduced us to Amin later on in the night when they had a chance, as it seemed he was shouting all the time, but in a jovial way. Hans butted in by saying 'This man is an English engineer who I am working with in Watia.'

Shaking hands I said 'We have met before, many years ago in England, Queen Elizabeth Barracks Crookham near Aldershot.'

Amin stared at me with such big eyes and he was frowning. After a minute or two he said.

'I remember you in the Medical Corps, Sergeant's Mess, you looked after me didn't you? It was a long time ago.'

'Yes, about twenty years I think.' I said.

'Enjoy yourself, I'll look after you now.' he laughed.

Back in Watia, the daily work was being carried out, but Zella was not his same flamboyant self, he realised he was in trouble, although he never to my knowledge saw Marchello. All I could think of was he must see him at week-ends as he always went to Tripoli. The men were very good at their own jobs now, and without hesitation we could leave them anytime. They all knew what to do and knew they would get extra pay. My flight was booked Halima drove me to the airport.

'Please come back' he pleaded as I went through to passport control. I had arranged a meeting with Brian as he was coming home to Manchester for a couple of weeks, he promised to phone me.

Joyce picked me up at Manchester with the kids.

'I have four weeks to make up my mind.' I told her.

We all went to Ibiza for a couple of weeks, and enjoyed a good hotel, food and weather.

When we got back there was a message to meet Brian at a hotel in Alderley Edge where we met him with his wife Christine. To my surprise there was another man with them, western dressed but I could tell he was Arab. He seemed to only talk to Christine. I got to dislike him and I ignored him the same as he did us, but it would not make any difference anyway.

'This Arab is very rude, what's his problem?' I later said to Brian.

'It's our landlord from Tripoli, Sourfraki's friend, it's a bit awkward I know, but what can I do, Christine seems to like him.' he said.

'I'd give him a kick up the arse and tell him to piss off' I thought. Later Brian gave me an envelope containing a contract, it was twelve weeks on, four weeks paid holidays. The space for an annual salary was left empty.

'Think it over, fill in the empty space and let me know' he said.

We said our goodbye's.

Joyce was quiet as we drove home, I asked if she was alright, she said she didn't like the company we had just left. 'Brian must be mad she's nothing but a prostitute' she said.

'Bloody hell Joyce, are you sure?' I said.

'I'm positive' she replied.

I asked Joyce about how she felt about me doing another twelve weeks in Libya.

Joyce said there was nothing going work wise here, but it was up to me, she would prefer me to find work at home, but she knew it would drive me mad with nothing to do and staying at home. So I phoned Brian.

'Thanks, I can put in for some English workers now, I've been holding back until I had your decision.' he said.

'If you are getting another gang of men, is there any chance of another engineer to help setting out, I know of a good lad if you are interested' I said.

'Yes, tell him he can start straight away, tell him to get in touch with Sid Hewitt he deals with all Sourfraki's contracts and will arrange all the air travel tickets.'

The lad I had in mind was my friend's son who worked with me at Staffordshire Public Works and was out of work and was not married so had no ties to think about.

Arriving back in Tripoli I was met by Halima, who was all excited to see me back and he told me there had been many changes while I had been away, but Brian would tell me back at the office.

'Good trip?' said Brian.

'Yes' I said shaking his hand.'I've made a start as regards to the workforce, half the Italians have left and you have ten British workers, sort it out and there will be another ten Brits on the way as soon as you give me the okay.' he said.

'What's Zella say?' I asked.

'Oh he's still there but not very happy he's your problem now'.

Back on site, it seemed as though I had never left, everything was the same the only thing different was the men. Zella organised a meeting that night and introduced me to the Brits who looked a tough lively bunch, some were overweight and some with beer bellies. 'God they won't last long' I thought. One fellow named Bryn seemed to be the most vocal, Zella had given me their C.V's and Bryn was a Rhodesian who had left because of the trouble with Mr. Smith's government.

'I left one Mr. Smith, Bryn said, 'it's seems as though I have another' he would remind me again many times later. He was an electrician/mechanic, married, and came from Cardiff. He was going to be in charge I thought immediately. There were two carpenters, four pipe layers, one looked older, a typical Irish labourer from Belfast but was living in Swansea. 'Owen O'Neil's my name, I've been a ganger on the roads' he said.

'And you'll be a ganger here as well Owen' I said.

Geordie said there was no guessing where he came from and had always worked with concrete what he didn't know about concrete wasn't worth knowing'

I told him he would be in charge of the Maggi Dutch mixer, and asked if he could drive.

'No' he said.

'I can' said a lad named Hardwick, his C.V. surprised me, a policeman with a question mark.

'Can you drive a concrete mixer lorry?' I said.

'Yes' he replied.

'Right the jobs yours.' I interviewed one more.

'Colley's my name' the man said, I've been out of work for twelve months and I'll do anything, I'm hoping you will give me a chance' he said.

I told him there would be no problem.

'As long as I know, it gives me time to find something, these are dangerous jobs working with the machines, lowering pipes into the trenches, and I only want experienced men there, is there anything you want to ask me?' I said.

'Yes, we've been here four days and hardly done anything, we just help the Italians' Bryn said. I told him to see me tomorrow morning at 6:00.am and I would sort it out. The chap with the beer belly named Webb said that the food was Italian pasta and rice all the time and asked if one of them could go in the kitchen to vary the food. 'Yes' I said 'the job's yours.' Everyone laughed.

'I take it you are all fixed up with accommodation?' I asked, there are four men to a trailer, two each side of the bathroom and you are to look after your own trailer, no one will clean up after you, so for your own hygiene, keep it clean.'

That night, while talking to Zella I was told that twenty two men had left but not any of the pipe gangs. That was going well. Next morning I introduced Soloman to Bryn as the Site Electrician and I told him he would come under his supervision. I told him to pick himself two men to help maintain the machines as they came in, and they were to be put under cover. All maintenance was to be done at night.

'The rest of the day is yours' I told them, 'but keep the machines working okay.'

Bryn and his men were never a problem and under difficult circumstances kept the machines, generators, and lighting and kitchen cookers going. The two Italian gangs were with Zahoor and his digger with Josef in the other. Halami was in the lorry with a man named Stan Peters, helping to load and unload the pipes. Said was up and down the site filling in behind the diggers, saving the diggers that work, they could carry on digging thus saving even more time. Brian had arranged the mixer with Hans, so I took Geordie and Hardwick to the concrete plant where Hans explained everything to them.

Hans turned to me. 'Brian tells me you are in total charge of all the contractors' he said 'so do we call you boss?'

'Yes' I said laughing. 'You *should* be in charge, he said. *you* are the only engineer on schedule, I've only got one more hanger to construct and then I'm off to Misrata to do the same, I'll probably see you when you become Area Manager.'

Zella was putting the levels in, that's all he had to do, and he was using my method with the stakes in the ground every twenty metres with a painted white strap on top and the pipe layer using the trammel. Mr. Lee, on the Korean site was about on schedule and could see things were getting better. The Korean workers always greeted me, which embarrassed me a little, as they always wanted me to stay for lunch or late dinner, and I was always making my excuses as I know they always ate dog. These dogs are a special kind of white Labrador which are always locked up in pens.

It had got to the stage where I could not keep refusing, I was too ashamed, so I accepted, saying I liked hot curry. The curry itself was that hot it burnt my mouth, so I drank plenty of water. I could not taste the meat so I cannot tell you what it tasted like. After that I had many meals with them. Their conditions were not as good as the other sites but they seemed happy enough. I only had one complaint all the time I was there, and that was that they were only allowed out of the camp once a month.

I asked why, but they shrugged their shoulders. Mr. Lee said Sourfraki could not supply transport.

'I'll look into it' I said, the other's go every weekend.'

I asked Zella, he said that the Arabs didn't like them because they ate dogs.

'Well, they don't taste too bad' I said, lying through my teeth.

Zella stared at me, mouth wide open, but he never said a word. Work was going very well since Hans had given me the old J.C.B. it must have been the only one in Libya, it was Sourfraki's anyway and now we had got a use for it. Bryn and his men soon got it going and were setting up another gang. Mr. Ram began to put in the duct pipe connections for the cables around the runway. Smiley from the Secret Police was always sniffing about, and I noticed he was being more friendly than usual.

'Mr. Smith' he said, is it possible for one of your trailers to be loaned to us as our guards on duty at the entrance to the camp have orders to be there all night, it is a twenty four hour duty now and there are four of them, two on, two off, so they will be able to sleep there,'

'Yes,' I said, but could you do a trade?'

'Such as' he said.

'Well, you have a bakery in the camp, could we buy bread from it instead of going to Azwara?'

He asked how much we would like and I told him about fifty loaves, they were like baguettes. He told me he would see about it. Later that day he came back all smiles and told me the deal was on, he told me Halima could arrange it with the baker Sergeant. Halima was very pleased, no more would he have to get up that early every night I told him to sort the finances out and let me know the cost.

That was a good job done and I was pleased with myself especially as the men had beautiful warm new bread for breakfast, which consisted of fruit juice, jams, and eggs, but no bacon or sausages after all, we were in Libya. Webb was getting a few stews and potatoes with vegetables, so everyone was happy. One of the Libyan lorry drivers offered me a bottle of Jonny Walker's whiskey for sixty dinars, which was around forty pounds in sterling, and for a treat I bought it and we played bingo one night, the full house being for the bottle. This went down well so we had one every weekend, while keeping watch outside for Smiley.

I think he knew, but as long it was inside our compound there was no problem. I wanted to see Juma so I asked Smiley to arrange it. He said Juma wanted to see me also the next day at 10:00am. Juma was pleased to see me and said that he had ten trailers coming in on site and could I connect them up with electricity and construct a septic tank to take the drains. He also wanted me to construct a concrete area with paths to each trailer he had drawn a plan which he showed me, I told him I would get on to it straight away.

'How many men have you under your contract now Mr. Smith?' he asked.

'Well, I said, with Mr. Lee's Koreans and Han's concrete plant it is around one hundred but I have had no time to calculate.'

'You have more men under you than I have and I am a Colonel, we'll have to call you The White Colonel.'

I said 'Yes, my hairs going whiter all the time.'

He asked where I had got my cap from, he had not seen one that colour before yellow, green and black.

'I had this given to me by Fidel Castro' I said.

That made my life much better in his eyes, he could not believe that I had worked In Cuba. 'Our leader is a very good friend of Castro and Che Guevara, perhaps you can help me' he said.

I told him I would try and get spares for his coaches and aircraft but up to now I hadn't any luck.

'I'll mention it, but the American's are watching everything that goes on as you know, wait until I tell them about you.' His mind was wandering away.

I told him I had noticed a small bus around the far side of the runway and I had been told that it belonged to him.

'Yes, it has been there since I've been here, something is wrong with it.' He said.

I asked him if I could see if I could get it going. He told me that if I could that I could have it. I told Bryn to take his men and see what they could do with it, and for any spares to see Halima. A week later and the twenty two seater bus was roaring around the airfield like a Ferrari.

I told Mr. Lee that this bus was for his men to go to Tripoli whenever they wanted, except Sundays of course, as this was the day that the British went. This worked wonders, but for myself it was a problem making excuses all the time as regards stopping for a meal. The next weekend I went to Tripoli and phoned Joyce. She told me everything was o. k.

Brian was not very happy, Fatalah, who was a director of Sourfraki's empire, who helped Brian with the administration side, asked Brian quietly, if he had a wife problem.

Brian did not offer a night at his place, so I left with Halima for Watia, but before I left he informed me that a firm called Southern Counties would arrive with two trailers, the accommodation for the four men who were to construct the water tanks that were to hold all the water that our pipes would collect around the airfields and roads. They were to operate by themselves, and would only come under my supervision inside the camp for accommodation and food.

After a couple of days they arrived, with ten more men from the UK. The fellow in charge of Southern Counties was called Pat Aust, who was very young and quiet and started to connect the two trailers with Bryn's help, as one of the trailers was for us. The ten men were brought up to the expected job situation and given their positions which Zella did not like, as one was a setting out engineer, he promptly packed his suitcases and left with four others, and I never saw him again. Although I was sorry to see them go I had the other Brits to consider. The name of the other engineer was Hywel, a short plump fellow with a Welsh shaky voice, he was to take Zella's accommodation.

Everything was going well, but unbeknown to me the men had set up a beer distillery, bringing in Boots own brew with labels on the tins saying Coffee and Bisto so as to get it through customs.

'I don't want to know.' I told Bryn and Geordie, but I did go to the tasting and it was bloody awful, but the men seemed to like it. The half dozen Italians brought out a bottle of wine that was more to my liking.

'You never offered me this before.' I said looking at them, 'No understand' they said laughing.

'Marchello is coming to see us tomorrow with our pay and then I think we will leave too, I'm very sorry.' Said Franko.

There was no Marchello that day so the rest of the Italians said they would leave at the weekend and go to Tripoli. On the Friday Fatella came to the site. I'd never seen him outside of the office.

'Mr. Roy,' as he always called me, 'I have bad news for you and the Italians' he said 'Will you call them.'

I told one of the men to bring the Italians in. As we were waiting, Fatella told me that Brian had left, and gone home.

'What about his wife and son?' I asked.

Fatella shook his head as the Italians came in, he then told them some grave news, Marcello had been found dead with his throat cut, and all the money, around seventy thousand dinars, about thirty five thousand pounds sterling was missing.

No one had been paid for last month, the Italians were in a fury, screaming and crying. Fatella said he would take them to Tripoli that day so I never saw any of them again. Hywel was a diamond, perhaps a little too zealous at times but I left him to it, thinking the heat would steady him. Juma came into my office the next day it was the first time he had been in our camp and was driving a Range Rover with Smiley as a passenger.

'Mr. Smith, I am sorry to interrupt your work he said, but it is important that I tell you that I am going to my old battalion, for as you know, I am a tank commander in the army, the new colonel is a pilot, although we are all army in Libya, you would in your country call him an RAF Officer, Smiley will introduce you to him in the next few days.'

He thanked me very much for all my help and said it had been a pleasure to see me and all the men at work.

One morning as we were working on the runway marking out the connections for the lights, a Range Rover travelling on the runway with headlights on came to us and stopped. An officer got out and asked for Mr. Smith.

'That's me' I said.

He introduced himself as Colonel Gabriel Alcadici, the new Commandant. I told him Juma had told me about him being a pilot. He asked me how things were, and I told him they were getting better after a slow start and I told him we would have his lights on in a few days. He seemed pleased and told me that if I wished to speak to him at any time I was not to hesitate as his door would always be open.

Mr. Ram, the Egyptian, came over asking what I thought of the new colonel. I told him I liked him and Mr. Ram said he was a good man, the best pilot in Libya. He went on to say that the colonel had been the only one to have shot another jet down but unfortunately it had been one of Mr. Ram's countrymen. Through Alcadici I used this camp more often using its library and his Cech doctor.

This came in very useful to me when anyone was ill or had an accident, it saved a two hour journey into Azwara, but I found out later that the men preferred to go to the hospital there as they had become very friendly with the nurses. One time a lad had been ill for a couple of days, his name was Dumpy and I thought he should go to see the doctor. Halima drove him, as sometimes the guards didn't like us Westerners, and would give us a bit of aggravation, but somehow they never messed with Halima, the big Turkish wrestler. When they got back Halima said the doctor had examined Dumpy and he was constipated he had not been to the toilet for days.

'He's given him some medication, so he should be o k' Halima said.

That night Hywel woke me up saying Dumpy was worse and could I take him to the army doctor.

'Yes, I said, get Halima and pick me up, I'll go with him.'

The guards stopped us, so I asked for the Colonel, they said he was asleep.

'Get him up I shouted, or let us through to the medical centre.'

Just then a Pakistani officer came to us, I'd seen him teaching the young Libyans to fly. He was a flight instructor and he waved us through and had got the doctor out of bed to see to Dumpy. He came back to us smiling along with the doctor and Dumpy and the officer said 'He is too embarrassed to say, but his medication is not to be taken orally, they are suppositories.'

'Bloody hell Dumpy I said, don't tell anyone, you'll never live it down.'

Whenever I saw Dumpy I always smiled. To my knowledge no one ever knew and I think he appreciated it. Pat Aust from Southern Counties seemed to be coping with his contract which was constructing the water tanks. This was connecting six hundred plates together with mastic in between to make them watertight and bolted together like a Meccano set. You could make them as long and wide as you liked with angle straps to stiffen and hold them in position. The floor was constructed the same way but no roof. All our pipes led to these tanks, so when it rained the water came to a smaller chamber with a pump inside which pumped the water into the tanks. There was one constructed tank on stilts, this would give pressure to over areas, the higher the more pressure. This four metre square high tank was filled with good drinking water piped from the existing water main in the army camp. Unfortunately, when it was filled it leaked like a sieve. This was a disaster and everyone laughed, which did not go down well with Alcadici or myself. I had left Pat and his men to their own abilities, thinking I was only responsible for their accommodation and food. It made no difference to Alcadici, he held me responsible. I told Pat to turn the water valve off.

'Don't let any more water in until it has been repaired.' I told him.

'How can we repair it when the water's out?' he said.

I told him to mark all the places outside and get a man inside the tanks in swimming trucks to see where it was leaking from and when the water had gone start gunning mastic in and tighten the bolts. It may have been with the heat at midday and the cold at night that had slackened them. After a few days filling and emptying every day, he got it watertight, but I began to worry about the big tanks around the perimeter and inside around the runway and also the fire hydrants, what if they leaked, there would be no water if there was an accident.

I told Pat to check and if he wanted more men then he was to tell me but we just could not take a chance on the other tanks leaking. I could tell they didn't like me interfering but if they didn't like it then they could get on their bikes. Their boss, a man called Roger Slater, who I had seen with Brian as he and his family lived next door, came to the site a few days later for the first time asking if everything was alright. I said it was now, but as you probably know Pat has had a problem unfortunately. He said he knew but also knew it had been resolved.

'Have you heard about Brian?' he said.

'Yes I said, Fatella came to tell me, but didn't explain why do you know what has gone on?'

'Christine went off to live with an Arab friend of Sourfraki's' said Roger.

'I did warn him but he took no notice' I replied.

Roger told me that Sid Hewitt was here with another fellow to help Fatella and he would like to see me if I could make it. That weekend I went to Tripoli and phoned Joyce and then went to the office.

Sid was talking to Fatella.

'Hello Roy, did you get through to UK?' he said.

'Yes after a while, it's a pain in the arse, half a day to make a bloody phone call.'

'Be careful what you say, you never know who is listening.' He said.

'Roy you are to take charge of all construction outside and Fatella the office, with help from Ernie.' He said.

Ernie came in, he was a slim fellow with hair swept back and was wearing glasses I was introduced to him as the Area Manager.

'You'll have Brian's Range Rover Sid said, and use of his flat in Tripoli when needed, also Ernie can have a room there if that's o k.'

I said there would be no problem. While I was in Tripoli I decided to take Halima, letting him drive the Range Rover with Said in the back to Sirte, which was about one hour's drive along a good road that leads to Benghazi. There was an airfield already there built by King Idris and we had men doing maintenance and renovation work to the Commandant's instructions. They looked a lazy lot and I asked who was in charge.

'I am' said a tall slim fellow with blond hair. I said I'd taken over from Brian and just looked at him, not offering my hand. I had taken an immediate dislike to this man and to the others, but maybe I was wrong but I thought I would test them.

'In the next few days a engineer will arrive with a couple of carpenters, he will take charge and three men will go to Watia to replace them' I said, will you send in your report to the office as there has been none from you for the last month.'

We were off to Misrata again, this was an old airfield just outside the Egyptian border.   We were extending the runways and taxi drives, some were laid in concrete and some in Tarmac and to my pleasure Hans was in charge.

'Hello boss' he said greeting me with a big smile, 'I told you you'd be boss.'

'Yes I said, how are you, is everything ok, is there anything you want?'

'No' he said, we are on the ball as you English say.'

I told him I had just been on the Sirte site and I was not happy. Hans told me he was not surprised as the men say they are always in Tripoli, so they are not doing much work.

'What does the Commandant say?' I asked.

'He's just the same, idle git.'

'Well, he must be signing the cheques or Sourfraki would be down here.'

'It's Sourfraki cousin, Hans said laughing, and by the way Amin always asked about you and there's some English people staying in the village making a film, one is named Oliver Reed, he can drink me under the table and I thought that was impossible.'

'Bloody hell Hans, I said, any chance of staying the night with you?'

'Yes, I am on my way now, come with me and I'll tell Halima where to pick you up in the morning, he's knows my place.'

Arriving at the holiday village I saw a crowd of people unpacking mini buses all carrying cameras and cases. The first man I recognised was Anthony Quinn, 'Bloody hell' I thought, and just behind him was Ollie. I strolled over with my Castro cap on holding my hand out to greet him, he just looked at me. His face I could see told me he was thinking who the hell was this man. I took my cap off and his face changed to a big smile.

'F—hell Smithy, I can't believe it' he said wrapping his arms around me and squeezing the life out of me.

For a while he just looked at me and kept saying he could not believe it.

'Of all places, in this God forsaken place and you turn up' he said.

'I bet you've got something in your room that I have not had for weeks?'

'Yes, he said. Tony, meet my old army friend.'

What a night we had, drink, you name it he had it, even Amin seemed to enjoy it.

The next morning I was woken by Halima who had made some coffee. It was 10:00 am, and Hans was still asleep as was Ollie and Tony. After coffee we drove back into Tripoli, I told Ernie to expect trouble from Sirte but not to worry. Lawson, my friend's son from the S.P.W days was to take over. I said goodbye to Sid and all, before driving off to Watia. Work was going well, Hywel was in complete control and so was Bryn, but Pat was getting aggro from his men, I think he had started to get a grip after they had let him down. One fellow I had spotted seemed to be miserable and complaining all the time.

 We only had enough potatoes for chips twice a week, and he thought they should have them every day. Potatoes seemed to be difficult to buy in Libya, I didn't know why and when you could get them they were very expensive, around twenty pound per bag sterling. This fellow I heard was going on strike, and he did with a couple more, so I went to see them and told them to pack their cases and leave the camp and they did, but later saw Pat drive out. He came back the next day asking me if I could fix him up with some men.

'No problem I said, Mr. Lee from the Korean site will fix you up and believe me Pat they will not let you down.'

Sourfraki asked me whether the Range Rover was as good as was advertised.

'Of course' I said, being British.

The Arabs always seemed to praise themselves, whereas I did not. The next thing I knew Sourfraki had bought two Range Rovers, one for himself and one for Brian, later I drove Brian's when he left.

To my shame both broke down with transmission trouble and were scrapped, forty thousand pounds gone just like that. Needless to say Sourfraki never asked my advice about cars again. Rumour had it Sourfraki had something to do with Marchello's death. It would not have surprised me because the way he was killed was the cowardly Arab way. One Sunday night, arriving later after a day in Tripoli the camp guards would not allow us in and this was upsetting the men and they began to shout at the guards to lift the bar which was across the road stopping our entry. Some even went to lift it themselves. The guards clicked their machine guns and started to fumble with them.

'They don't know how to fire them.' Shouted Bryn, and went over took one of the weapons off one of the guards and disassembled it and them put it back together again and fired a couple of shots in the air.

'Bloody hell Bryn, don't show them how to kill us you bloody fool,' shouted Geordie.

Hearing the shots, more guards came out of the trailer which I had given them. Smiley was amongst them.

'What is the problem Mr. Smith?' he asked.

'Smiley, get these guards to allow us in or I'll tow that trailer away and we'll sleep in it ourselves.'

I could hear women screaming inside, and Smiley looked worried. He then shouted to the guards in Arabic to lift the bar which they did and we went through to our camp. Smiley never mentioned the incident again but I later found out why we were not allowed in or out after dark, they did not want to see lorries loaded with large crates which were stamped 'Made in Pakistan.' These all went along the road at the far end of the runway which was always guarded. Hans told me they were building a massive plant that was very secretive, and at night a large carrier plane would land and its load travelled along that road and there were land mine signs everywhere.

'I think you know what it is' Hans said to me.

'It's nuclear,' I thought.

The problem I had with Pat Aust's men after the leaking water tower was not fully told as I had fisticuffs with the little mouthy one who wanted the men to go on strike unless there were chips on the menu every day. I ask you, in the middle of the Saraha Desert, one hundred and twenty degrees, going on strike because there were no chips, people would not believe it but it was true. I felt it was up to me to put him right as some men were getting very angry and it might have got out of hand and I didn't want to lose any of my men. This reminded me of the barometer incident. Every now and again, if the temperature got to one hundred and twenty degrees worked stopped, but some crafty bugger kept hanging it in the sun, instead of in the shade

Later Pat said it was much better with the men from the Korean site and things were much more pleasant. I told Pat that I didn't put up with that sort of aggro and it was best to nip it in the bud straight away as it would get you down and this God forsaken desert was no place to be unhappy. My twelve weeks was up and I was looking forward to four weeks at home. Some other men who had done six months were also going home with two weeks holiday with pay. These men were on twelve months contract with two weeks holidays after six months. We had a good time on the Caledonian Airways flight, you could have as much as you could drink and I'm afraid quite a number did. As we arrived at Gatwick one lad was in a trolley with his mate Webby carrying his case. Dumpy was running through the doors with the customs men following him shouting 'Hey, where do you think you are going?'

'Tonypandy' shouted Dumpy not stopping, with the door closing behind him.

I made my way to transit as I was flying to Manchester, I remembered thinking how many of these men will return? I had four weeks off with the family and we had two weeks in Corfu. Time soon went by and I was soon back in Watia and to my surprise everyone had returned. I remember thinking what a great bunch of men they were, I could not have wished for better. Something that had been going on unnoticed was the shelves in the recreation rooms were filling with books that the men had brought, and when they had read them they were putting them on the shelves. We had quite a library.

I brought aircraft books which I knew the pilots liked, and any English books they had they passed on to us and vice versa with the American camp in the oil fields. This is where I started to read, I had never bothered before, the only books I had ever read until then was 'Mill on the Floss' which was a prize for coming top of my class at school, and 'The Man in the Iron Mask.' My favourite books at present were Wilbur Smith books from the American camp. I don't know why I had not seen them before also James Michener who wrote South Pacific, my favourite musical. How funny this became to me in later years as I was reading as many as four books a week, so after one year it mounted up to over two hundred books. I had to stop this addiction as I was forgetting what I had read. When I was in the army a coloured lad came to the mess, he had been sent to do punishment and I set him on cleaning and polishing the dining room floor. He was a very talkative lad but pleasant enough and he said he was clairvoyant and could read the future. I told him to go away and do his work but he kept saying things that interested me. He told me I had had a very difficult childhood, but for me life was beginning to change. He told me the people I was going to meet and places I was going to were only granted to so many people. He said our lives were already mapped out for us and there was nothing we could do about it. He also told me that I was going to do things and see things that not many of us see and do. I thought 'rubbish' but one thing was right, I had married the most beautiful girl in the world.

Why I have mentioned the above is because one morning Alcadici stopped and asked me if I would like to have a fly around.

'Oh, I said, is it ok? I've never flown in anything like this before.'

The men started shouting 'go on boss, go on.'

I was in the Range Rover I smiled and nodded then drove to the other end of the airfield where the Jets were.

'We will go in the trainer Mirage' said Alcadici.

I got in the front by the nose. Alcadici was behind and was seated a bit higher. One of the lads put my head gear on and mask and said pointing to the head gear and mask 'breathe oxygen.' He asked me if everything was ok and I gave him the thumbs up.

Alcadici asked me if I could hear him. I said I could and then we were off.

The noise I was expecting never came, it was silent as we went down the runway. My men were waving, I'm sure all the camp had arrived to see me off. Suddenly there was a roar, and my head went back onto my seat, what an experience, I'd never felt the power of anything like this before, sand dunes were flashing past me I could see the road to Azura and in a matter of minutes we were over the Mediterranean. God this is unbelievable I thought, and sweeping down, we circled and went back into the desert where we saw about twenty to thirty tanks.

'Juma, Alcadici said, we will go down and give him a wave' which he did.

'How are you Smith?' Alcadici asked.

I told him I was amazed and I had never experienced anything so wonderful.

He told me he flew every morning and had the same feeling every time he flew.

The landing was a bit frightening, it's seemed that we were going too fast to land but I never felt a thing. I thanked Alcadici and said I'd never forget the experience. He told me it had been his pleasure. A lot of the men had heard about my flight and came to the edge of the runway to see me, so I had plenty of witnesses to me flying in a fighter Mirage jet. The clairvoyant's tales were beginning to come true.

Stan Peters the buyer, was as usual going round to see if any of the men wanted anything from Azura.

'Hi Stan I said, I see you do a bit of running at night.'

'Yes he said, my father was the marathon runner Jim Peters.'

I said I remembered him twenty yards from the tape when he collapsed, otherwise he would have won a gold medal and that was a great shame. I asked Stan if he was alright and he said he was fine.

Everything was going like clockwork there were no problems so I started to travel to the other sites more often and Lawson at Sirte was fine. Some of the men had left, which I had already told Ernie about and Hans was up to date on everything. One other contract came our way which was to connect trailers on Juma's tank camp which we carried out in about two weeks.

My time was nearly up and some of the old gangs were leaving. My wife was under the doctor, she was not well so I decided my time was up, Lawson and Hywel could finish off what was to be done. There was one meeting in Watia that I attended before leaving on the night we switched on the lights for night flying. Mr. Ram was pleased, we were only three weeks behind schedule so it was not too bad. Apart from one or two bulbs not coming on it was a success and we all went to the Officer's mess. Gaddafi was there with a man I now know as Arafat along with Juma, Alcadici and Major Mubruk. There were quite a few others there, Mr. Lee, Hans and many more that I could not name. To my embarrassment they had bought me a going away present, a book signed by Gaddafi about Libya which I keep with my conch from Castro.

I said my goodbye's to everyone, especially to Halima, Said, Zahoor, Josef, Soloman and Jamba. They presented me with a lovely piece of Ivory. I had a lump in my throat but I was beginning to get home sick. I was longing to see Joyce and I was dying to taste again my favourite local Oatcakes*. Something also told me that I was wanted at home so off I went.

*An Oatcake is a delicacy local to the Potteries and the North Staffordshire area. It takes the form of a pancake, and is eaten locally in great quantities with savoury fillings. Its recipe's are closely guarded secrets,handed down from generation to generation and are sometimes taken to the grave.

London 1982-1984

I was enjoying my time at home with my wife and children I had missed them more than I thought. Joyce was a little anaemic so the doctor said, but he would keep an eye on her otherwise she was o. k.

Julie my eldest had bought a new one bedroom house and seemed to be enjoying herself. Karen, my second eldest had got married and bought a house at a place called Westbury, about two miles from us. The twins were no problem although I noticed Jeremy becoming 'Joyce's boy' as they say. I had been busy doing work on the homes of the girls, getting my house and garden in good condition and also building a conservatory at the back of the house. All this time I noticed my salary was still going into my account from Sourfraki, and I was thinking it's their fault, I'm not objecting to their mistakes, anyway I suppose they will be ringing me one day.

Sure enough about a week later Sid Hewitt was on the phone.

'I thought you would be ringing about my salary still going into the bank.' I said.

'No it's not that, Sid said, Sourfraki insists you are on sick leave and must be paid, I'm ringing about a position that has come up in London and he wants you to run it, it's looking after his property in London, he and some other Arabs are buying as much property that comes on the market, and he wants you to supervise all repairs, extensions and alterations, he asked if you would come down one day and have a look around.'

I told him I would be down the next week.

'We will meet in the Cavendish Hotel on Jeremy Street, look forward to seeing you.' Sid replied.

Waiting in the Cavendish, Sourfraki, who had seen me come in stood up and shook my hand.

'Roy, nice to see you.' he said.

That was the first time he had called me by my Christian name.

'You know Sid, and these are my colleagues.' Sourfraki said.

There were no names but I knew them as Mr. Kosonggoi the arms dealer and Mr. Al. Habtoor the racehorse owner. I had seen them on T.V. many times. Another man came to me later, a Mr. Gordon the architect and was introduced.

'As Sid has already told you, Sourfraki said, we would like you to supervise all our properties, Mr. Gordon has drawn up all the necessaries and a bill of quantities, would you be able to give us an estimate so we can budget the finances?'

Mr. Gordon produced two drawings and spoke about the properties, one was a flat at St, Johns Wood opposite the Lords cricket ground, the other was a flat at Kensington next to the fire station.

The third property which was the largest project was 37 Avenue Road, St. John's Wood. This is the road from Swiss Cottage to Regents Park, a very desirable house next to the American Embassy. The other property was at Shiplake, a small village next to Henley-on-Thames.

'I have only had the information for a few days and I am still working on the drawings and getting planning permission.' Mr. Gordon said.

Sourfraki said we did not have time to look at all the properties but he would like me to see 37 Avenue Road and said he would drive us round, us being Sid, Mr. Gordon and myself. The Arabs nodded as they said their goodbyes and left the meeting. Sourfraki paid for the coffees and asked for his car to be bought round to the front entrance. As we went outside there was a Rolls Royce with a license plate H.M.S. 009. Sourfraki got in the driver's seat with Mr. Gordon in the front passenger seat with Sid and myself in the back. The car had tinted glass so no one could see inside.

'Bloody Hell Sid, with this number plate they will think we are royalty,' I said.

'Some Police do, they come to attention and have waved us through many times.' Sid said, laughing.

We drove around Regents Park and turned into Avenue Road stopping at number 37.

'Roy, said Sourfraki, I wanted to knock this down and rebuild it like my home in Tripoli which you worked on but Mr. Gordon tells me it has a conservation order on it and that makes it impossible, but my lawyer is looking into it, there is no doubt in my mind that you will not be allowed to do that but inside the house you can do what you want.'

Sourfraki told me that my first job would have to be the demolition of the front walls as he would have to park his car on the road which would cause a lot of aggro with traffic. He said he would like two double electric gates so as to be able to drive in and out. The drive was the shape of a half moon which cut the garden down but Sourfraki said he did not mind that. I asked him if this was going to be his own house and he replied it was, unless he was offered a price that he could not afford to turn down.

'He's paid £860,000 for this Roy, Sid said, and he wanted to knock the bloody thing down' he said shaking his head.

Sourfraki asked if I was able to take the project on. I said I was but I would like to take the drawings and quantities home and give some kind of costing. He told me to make it as soon as possible and said it was no use going inside the property as he wanted to demolish it all. I spent a week on the drawings, getting prices and organising any labour that would be willing to live in London.

There is no doubt the Potteries men are renowned for good tradesmanship, but always found it difficult to work away from home. The building trade was going through a difficult time, so I was able to get most of the men I wanted. There were twelve in all, bricklayers, joiners, plasters, plumbers and electricians with a couple of labourers who would be willing to put their hands to anything. They would be paid hourly, much more than in the Potteries and it would be tax free plus accommodation, all they had to supply was a sleeping bag and their personal tools and would also buy their own food and drink, especially the latter.

From the drawings, I estimated £450,000 to do all the construction work but the finishing, such as kitchens, bathrooms and fireplaces etc then Sourfraki would be responsible. I phoned Sid who said I had underestimated, Gordon said the same, maybe my price would be correct in the Potteries but obviously not in London, especially St. John's Wood. I said I would go through it again and managed to raise it to £600,000. I re-thought this again and put another £100,000 so my final estimate came to £700,000 plus Sourfraki's finishings. Sourfraki told me he would budget me to that amount and I would be responsible for paying and keeping accounts. He said he would see that I got permission to withdraw from the Nat West bank in St. Johns

Wood, and I was to let him know when I was starting. He assumed we were going to use the house as a base and he would arrange for me to have the keys. I asked Bill to get the men ready for Monday and organise a mini bus for him to pick up and I said I would see him at 6:30 am on Monday morning at my house as it was on the way to the M.6 motorway. I told Danny to pick up his men and then leave the car at my garage, as I took it they would be going in the eight seater Peugeot. John, the electrician and Phil, the plumber would go in their own vans as they had a lot of equipment and directions had been given.

On Monday morning outside number 37 we met a man who I was told was Alan the gardener. He had the keys to the property. Sourfraki had gone overseas and would be back in two weeks he had also given Alan an envelope, in it was a cheque book and an introduction letter for the bank manager. I instructed the men that our accommodation was the top floor which housed four bedrooms and two bathrooms. I would be staying on the second floor and I told them to sort themselves out. Within an hour all the men had turned up and there were no problems on the M.6. We began demolition after having a sandwich and a drink for lunch. A skip had arrived and was directed to the rear of the property which was in Townsend Road. That would be the main entrance to the building as the men had started taking the front wall down and excavating the new driveway.

Soon as this is done the better I thought, as vehicles calling would not interfere with traffic. John was taking all the old wiring out and supplied us a temporary supply. The telephone had been re-connected and Phil was sorting out the plumbing and central heating down in the cellar/basement as this was where most of the work was to be done, as it was to become the kitchen and dining areas. There was also to be a bathroom with a sauna next to it, behind that would be a gas boiler large enough to heat the whole house.

Walls were being knocked down but there were no new walls inside to be built as Sourfraki wanted larger rooms. We had done a very good weeks work, and the men seemed to enjoy themselves especially going out at night as some had never been to London before. Sourfraki was back the next week, he seemed happy but I could see he didn't like the dust and dirt. John the electrician wanted more information about light and plug switches etc, so I mentioned to Sourfraki that it maybe to his advantage to have a word with him.

'No, he said quite strongly, the men must not know who I am, I don't like to be known to anyone but you.'

Strange, I thought, how can I keep him secret, the men already know him. I mentioned this to Sid when he phoned to ask how things were going.

'Yes, he's been to Tripoli and Gaddafi has told him he's spending too much time overseas and if he's not careful he'll be on the black list.'

'What's that?' I asked.

'You don't want to know, answered Sid but it's very important.'

After another couple of weeks things were going to schedule but we then had a visit from the conservation and building inspectors. Two well dressed university 'penguins' as we later called them.

'Stop the work' one said.

'You lads carry on working I'll tell you when to stop work here.' I said.

I then asked who they thought they were. They told me they were the building inspectors and had not been notified and we should not have started work without their say so. I told them that our architect had told us to start and told them if they didn't mind they were to leave the premises and discuss it with him.

'You can't demand us to leave' one said.

'See these men off the site' I said.

Danny and a few of the big lads made a move to them and the 'penguins' turned and left. I phoned Mr. Gordon to tell him what had happened.

'Not to worry, he said, I'll look into it, they should inform me when they are coming to site so I can arrange to be there.'

Next day the same two men arrived but didn't come on to the site they waited outside for about ten minutes and then Mr. Gordon arrived, they were talking about the front wall and drive and after a while they came into the existing study which I had turned into my office. Mr. Gordon took me to one side. 'Roy, you know who these people are and they would like to see the drawings,' which I showed them.

'There it shows a double drive and you have seen the dropped kerbs, we've done nothing different have we Roy?' Mr. Gordon said.

'No, I answered, but there was only one single gate if I remember, have you a drawing in your office showing that?'

'No, we have the same as you' they said.

'Well, if there was only one single gate, the people before must have done it without your permission.'

'Gentlemen, I think that is correct.' said Mr Gordon.

We won the day, but I knew this would come back on me later and they would make things difficult for me, which they did. The things they made us do would have bankrupted a small builder, we were lucky having Sourfraki. The 'penguins' visited the site weekly but only when accompanied by Mr. Gordon who told me if there was anything different to the drawings only the materials were to be altered such as angle irons over all windows and doorways were to be stainless steel. This of course trebled the cost. Also they were to be bolted onto the concrete lintel behind. This had to be drilled at the factory and bolted on with stainless bolts. Builders we got to know in the local pubs had never heard about stainless, they were taking the micky and I should have told them where to go but I held my tongue, it would have made matters worse.

After a couple of months things started to take shape and Sourfraki was coming on site two or three times a week. He had started to talk to John the electrician about dimmer switches, burglar alarms, camera's etc, he seemed to be taking an interest in the job now the dirt and dust had gone.

'Roy, tomorrow I will take you to see some bathroom suites and kitchens, I will tell you what I want and you make a list and buy them later at a reduced price.' The next day we drove to Harrods and parked outside as though we were royalty and a man dressed in a green uniform and top hat opened the door for *me*, a hairy arsed bricklayer from the Potteries, who would have believed it. Inside I followed Sourfraki around making notes of names and prices. We were joined by a man who I now know as Al – Fayed. He talked to Sourfraki as we walked around, they seemed to be good friends, he was one of the Cartel buying property, though I did not know this at the time. Around two hours later we said our goodbyes and drove to Selfridges. We again looked around pricing and changing some things from Harrods until Sourfraki decided that was it.

The Jacuzzi that was to go in the master bedroom would be coming with the marble steps, floors and kitchen top from Italy within the next week or two. The kitchen units were coming from Germany, the only thing he had not decided on were the chandeliers and mesh in front of the radiators. As Sourfraki was telling me all this I made the necessary notes. When we got back I told Bill all about what had happened he asked if this was real or were we on Candid Camera and he would go and have a look to see if the T.V. vans were outside. Work was going well, the scaffolding was coming down as the roof and chimney had been repaired and new guttering and downspouts had been fitted. The brickwork had been cleaned with powerful hoses, it looked like new and the dirty stoned blocks on each corner of the building plus the columns and pillars around the balconies and stairs up to the front door had come up beautiful. The front walls were capped with white stone coping, and the drive was tarmacced in red and looked magnificent from across the road.

Mr. Kossonggoi and his wife who lived across the road said it was like a new building and they thought we had excelled ourselves. When I told Sourfraki he was really pleased, I also mentioned his wife was also admiring it and I said I thought I knew her. He told me she used to be married to King Farouk, she was Queen Soraya. Sourfraki smiled, he must have seen my face.

'Guess what Bill' I said.

'No more please, I can't believe all this, pinch me' he said.

One of the workers named Steve I noticed, started to have the odd day or two off. I asked Bill what his problem was and where does he stay, as I knew he came from Chell in the Potteries

'I'm sorry to say but he's got in with the wrong crowd, we've all warned him about them but he takes no notice.'

'Is he drinking too much?' I asked.

'It's not the drink, he's on drugs' said Bill.

'Bloody hell Bill, I've heard about these drugs but I've never come across anybody who uses them, just keep an eye on him and I'll do the same.'

Phil the plumber had got on well, and was ready for the bathrooms. I gave him the list and he said he could get the same from the Potteries at half the price as Twyfords are from the Potteries and we could get the tiles from H.R. Johnson.

'Whatever you save I'll see you get half.' I said.

At the weekends he brought the necessary things down and I would give him the signed cheques and everybody was happy.

One morning I noticed Steve behind the mixer, he was concreting the patio floor he looked terrible. I shouted him to come into the office as I wanted to talk to him.

'I'm sorry but I'll have to let you go I said, something is wrong with you.'

'I'm alright.' He replied.

'No you're not, one day you will thank me for getting you away from here, you can stay till Friday but you will not be needed again.'

I told Danny not to pick him up on Monday but to pick up Frank, the wall tiler instead, he could start the bathrooms. As we were working on all the floors it became a problem living there as well, so I spoke to Sourfraki about getting bed and breakfast for the men. It was no problem as he had just bought a couple of hotels and one at Paddington, The Redlands Hotel. Sourfraki said this would be just the place but he would like two men to stay here as we don't want any break-ins again. He said to tell Glyn to put the cost of room and breakfast *only* on his account as there was a bar there.

I told him I would like my wife and children to come down for a few days and he told me to take them to The White House Hotel off Regents Park, he had a suite there and we could have it anytime as long as I informed Josef the manager. Joyce and the twins came down quite a lot after that, it seemed to pick her up a bit, as I noticed she didn't look too well. I asked if she had seen a doctor and she said she had and he had sent her to hospital to attend Mr. Ibbotson's Clinic, he said there was something wrong with her blood. Joyce continued to say that she was anaemic and had been given some tablets and would have to have a blood test every two or three months, she had a lack of iron.

Joyce and the children would, after breakfast go to somewhere different every day. I would go to Avenue Road and they would meet me there in the afternoon. The lorry was to arrive with the marble from Italy on Sunday so I and two other lads who said they would work that weekend unloaded it and the weekend after the kitchen arrived along with the jacuzzi. Bill and Phil stayed that weekend, I had not mentioned the break in before but it was upsetting as when I reported it to the St. John's police station they arrived two days later.

Stephen, the only local lad I had working for me (actually, he was a scouser) said he knew who it was, the two men who had come and asked for a job.

'Can you remember when you asked what they did they answered, well what do you require?'

'You said you were looking for electricians and plumbers,'

'That's what we are then.' They said very conveniently and you told them 'on your bikes.'

John and Phil, who had had some tools stolen asked Stephen if he knew them. He said they used the same pub as we do and he would point them out to us tonight. The word went round we were all going to the Swiss Cottage Pub that evening. Next morning one lad arrived with a cut over one eye and another with a bandaged hand. When the police arrived I thought it was about the break-in that I had reported. They said they did not know anything about that, they were making enquires about the fracas outside the local pub. I said we did not know anything about that. Danny said that he did not know anything either and Bill also said that he did not know what they were talking about.

'Well, I said, it's seems you don't know about the break-ins and we don't know about the fracas.'

They looked around and said 'very nice' and left.

Sid phoned saying there was another cheque book at the bank. There was another company's name on it and I was to pay for anything that Sourfraki had sent to you and I was to keep it on a separate account, I was not to get it mixed up with my accounts.

Danny had done well, as I had left the other smaller jobs to him. The flat at St. Johns Wood was complete and fully re-decorated. I used the same company Regent's Deco for Avenue Road. They were two married couples, they were good and their prices were fair, the only problem that bothered me was the language, but the lady had heard it all before, people down here did not seem to care like we would in the Potteries. Dave, who had done all the plastering, left the site so I only had to get in touch with the company to do the fibrous work. This entailed cornices, centre pieces and arch coves in some of the walls where John had leads for a light inside. Al Habtoor called with Sourfraki, he was more than delighted and said that he was building a hotel and leisure area in Jordon by the Dead Sea and he was looking for a project manager to take control of finishings and did I know anyone.

'Yes, I said, my old boss from Cuba Alan Walsh, but he has been poorly, he calls here from time to time, he is helping John the electrician with cameras for security, I'll mention it to him.'

'Good, ask him to give me a call here's my card said Al Habtoor.'

Soufraki asked how the marble was, I said it was beautiful and his measurements were spot on.

That bought a smile, especially with Al Habtoor being there.

That will cost you another rise boss I thought.

Mr. Gordon came on site, I had not seen him for a few weeks. He brought another man with him who he introduced as Mr. Ireson, the chief planning officer for Westminster.

'I believe you had a few run-ins with my assistance' he said.

I nodded.

'You know these are the fellows who are taking over, I suspect you, like me come from a trade background, I'm a joiner, by the look of outside I would guess you know about stone masonry and brickwork. I told him I had served my trade as a bricklayer.'

'You didn't want to knock this house down did you?' he asked.

'No' I replied.

I told Mr. Gordon that all the other properties had been completed and Avenue Road was coming to completion and I would have to start laying off the men. I was hoping Shiplake at Henley would be ready. He said it was but he had not been paid for all the drawings in London yet. I asked him, where was his invoice as I had not seen it. He looked at me rather strangely and said he had sent it to Sid. I told him he should have given it to me as I was responsible for all payments regarding the London's properties. He said he had a reminder on him and he was hoping to see Sid that day. I told him he could give it to me and I would pay him as Sid was overseas and it would be a week or more before he would be back. We went to the office and he gave me the invoice which was for £8,000. I wrote the cheque and the invoice was paid. He looked delighted, I think he was struggling financially.

I asked if I could start at Fairacre. That was the name of the property at Shiplake. Mr. Gordon told me to give him a call when I was ready as he only lived about half an hour's drive away in Reading. I had asked Sourfraki about the fibre plastering as we were ready about a week before. He came with a brochure from T.O. fibre Plaster Company.

'These are the people I would like to do the job, but get a quote and get them down, they are pretty pricey if you don't' said Sourfraki.

When I phoned them they said they would come that afternoon as they were only a few miles away in Romford. They arrived one fellow in a blue suit and another in a white boiler type suit. I showed them around, telling them what I required. As far as they were concerned it was for me, we kept away from saying the property was owned by Arabs as the price always doubled when mentioned but they were not daft, they knew. As I was showing the boss, as I called him, around, Bill was talking to the man in the white suit. I heard Bill tell him we had come down from the Potteries as there was little work there.

'I've got everything down, I will work out a quote and let you have it tomorrow' he said.

I had been looking at their brochure and saw that they did a bar. I asked if it was in plaster with the columns and pillars. I was told that they priced everything in plaster but you had to pay extra for the bar top as you may require wood or marble, plaster was not suitable. They also made plastic columns for external use. I asked how much the bar would cost without the top and was told we were talking about £4,500. When they had gone Bill told me they had no work, they were very slack and we may be able to get a fairer price. I thanked Bill for the info.

Frank the tiler was helping Bill and others laying the marble floors in the basement, hallway and outside steps to the front door. The quarry tiles in the outside patio were completed. When everything was done I was going to take Bill and Danny to Shiplake. The man from the plaster company came the next morning with a quote of £4,500 for the bar which I knew about and £9.500 for the rest which was £14,000 in total. I told him that was too much and I was thinking about £10,000 tops. He said he couldn't come down that low but he could come down £1,000 and that would be his rock bottom.

'I'll meet you halfway at £12,000 I said, and I'll pay half when you deliver the materials and the rest on completion so you will not be standing out of money and you can start tomorrow.'

He said he would have to speak to his office which he did and told me they could start the next day and we had got a bargain, and he was sure we would make a profit.

The only problem I had at that time was that my best joiners were having difficulty in constructing a fluted piece from the ceiling overhanging the Jacuzzi in the master bedroom suite.

It had to be in plywood to give it the proper shape and then Frank had to tile it in mosaic. Sourfraki would say it's not right and Colin and Derek would have to start again but never complained until Sourfraki said it was perfect, they were also responsible for the wardrobes, all mirror fronts and all the radiators apart from the top floor which were to be boxed in with a golden colour mesh with little stars on each in front of all the radiators to let the heat out.

Frank was finishing the mosaic on the flute and John had fixed spotlights in it and around the room. The floor and steps to the Jacuzzi were in marble, the walls and the rest of the ceiling were in mirror tiles. Sourfraki kept moving the spotlights around much to John's annoyance. Frank said that all we wanted now was Marilyn Monroe in the jacuzzi and we would be laughing. They had never seen anything like this before but I had, it was the same as Sourfraki's home in

Tripoli. As the fibre plasters finished in each room the decorators moved in as I had accepted their quote and as they completed the carpet people laid the floors. This came under Sourfraki as it was not in my quote so I paid out with the other cheque under the name SU properties. I could spare Bill and Danny now, so I took them down to Shiplake with me where we met Mr. Gordon who was already waiting for us. He had his wife with him I would say they were in their seventies. He had retired years ago and only did the odd drawing now and again. He came in touch with Sourfraki through Sid, who was a distant cousin. He gave me the keys to the property then showed us around.

 Sourfraki had paid £600,000 for this property about one year before and had already turned down a bid of one million for it. Mr Gordon asked if I knew he had turned down three million for Avenue Road from the U. S. Embassy. He had only paid £800,000 for it two years before. Property was going sky high, especially in London. Mr. Gordon must get all this information from Sid I thought. The property we were looking at was a bungalow and our job was to take the roof off and build on top to turn it into a four bedroom house. The roof tiles were shingle, which are not ordinary tiles but made from cedarwood. These would have to be taken off and stacked carefully as they would be re-used. The swimming pool had to be demolished and re-built larger with a proper roof on so it would be not outdoors like it was. The tennis court was to be re-laid, it had gone wild. The lawns went down to the side of the Thames where there was a landing stage that needed a lot of repair. The boathouse was also to be renovated. There was a six seater motor boat inside so we had to be careful. The drains were to be altered and connected to a septic tank with a Macerater inside. This was because the area was classed as a flood area, and by law it would have to have one.

Over by the entrance was a cottage or lodge, it had two bedrooms and was fitted out for us to use but there were to be no alterations there at this time. I asked Bill and Danny if there was anything they wanted to ask while Mr. Gordon was here.

'What about the foundations Bill asked, taking the extra weight?'

I was glad that he asked the question because it was a most important job and we would have the building inspectors on at us all the time but not as bad I hoped as those at Avenue Road. We would have to undercut every other metre down to the existing foundations, and then twelve inches below the concrete but we could not concrete ourselves until the inspector had passed it. When we had gone all the way round we would have to start digging out the metre in-between where we had already concreted it so we would need a pump.

'As you can see you will be below the Thames and it's my experience that water will start to come in as you start digging' said Mr. Gordon.

We said goodbye to him and his wife as they left and we had another good look round. The services were not on or the phones, so this would have to be chased up before we started. We timed how long it took to get back and it was around three quarters of an hour or a little more depending on the traffic at certain times. Everything at Avenue Road was fine, and Bill and three of the men had gone to Shiplake as all services were back on. Bill had a price for the scaffold to be erected all around and a roof scaffold on top to protect the existing rooms when we took off the roof. I told him to get another price and then to choose who he thought was the most suitable, which he did.

Alan Walsh came on site and I told him about Al. Habtoor and asked if he felt up to it. He said he was, and going there might help him as Yola and his two sons had left him. I gave him the card and off he went, it was to be twelve months before I spoke to him again. John was fixing the cameras outside as Sourfraki was inside adjusting the T.V's. Eventually he was satisfied with everything so John went to Shiplake to do the same as here but we were to keep the lodge in it's originally condition and it was to be our working supply. I told John the phone was working so he could keep in touch if need be. There were only five Potteries lads left, the others were contractors, decorators and plasterers. Phil the plumber had completed, and everything was working. There were no leaks, and the central heating was working, so the only job now would be the coupling of the kitchen sinks when the joiners had fixed them. This was a slight problem as the men had not worked on this kind before, the sink unit and cooker were in the middle of the kitchen with all services to them from under the floor.

'Never seen anything like this' they kept saying.

'I have, I said tongue in cheek, 'in Hollywood.'

The marble top fitted perfectly and so did the marble on the bar. Sourfraki certainly knew his marble as the lads said.

'You'll have to tell him that and he'll give you a rise' I said laughing.

To my surprise they did just that, much to Sourfraki's ego. As the weeks went by I started to have a few days in Shiplake. The scaffold was up, the roof was off and the underpinning was going well. It was a good job that we had got the water pump as there was water everywhere we dug.

One afternoon, five weird looking lads came on site, long hair down to their shoulders and unshaven.

'Bloody hell Bill, I said, for god's sake don't set them on'

Bill burst out laughing 'sorry lads, he said, I cannot set you on.'

'Why?' said one of the lads laughing.

John said to me 'you don't know who they are, do you? they are the famous rock group Deep Purple, they live next door.'

'They are all millionaires' he said laughing.

'Stick your f.....g job where the sun don't shine' shouted one.

The lads never let me forget it, even in the Potteries they got to know how square I was. Joyce was getting no better and I began to fear the worst. I told her I would go to the hospital with her next time. I had a few days off and went with her to see Mr. Ibbotson. First she had a blood test and waited about an hour for the results, then Mr. Ibbotson called us in again, he said the results were not very good.

'I have leukaemia don't I?' she said.

Mr. Ibbotson said she had had it for maybe three years but she was not to worry as he was treating patients like Joyce that had been ill for ten years or more.

'Why wasn't I told before?' she asked.

'Because you never asked, and I am not advised to say anything unless requested' he said.

I was speechless, the shock was affecting my legs and knees the same as before. We went home not saying a word, how I drove home I don't know but I collapsed on the settee. I could not stop crying with her, after all the hard work we were beginning to enjoy the good times now this had happened.

The twins were about to return home from school so we pulled ourselves together and decided we would carry on as normal.

Back at Avenue Road things were nearly completed, Sourfraki was bringing people in all the time, he was very proud and people were really impressed. One day he arrived with three other men all in Saville Row suits, Sid was one but the other two I could not quite recognize them, they stared at me and smiled.

'Bloody hell' I thought, it's the Colonels Juma and Alcadici, I grabbed and shook their hands.

'I thought I knew you but could not recognize you out of uniform.' I said.

They said I looked the same and they had heard good reports about me. I could not get over seeing them it was a good job there was no T.V. about as Libya was not getting very good press at the time. Juma and Alcadici said they were staying at the Dorchester and asked if I could get along one night, to which I said I could. I cornered Sid and asked if Sourfraki was still in the black book.

'No, he answered, he's not anymore as he has offered this property as the Libyan Embassy or the Ambassador's residence, and guess who will be the Ambassador?' he said looking at Sourfraki.

'Say no more' I said.

I told Sid they had invited me to the hotel and I asked him if he thought I should go. Sid said I must and the only thing I had to put on was a tie. That night I arrived at the Dorchester. Colin and Derek dropped me off wearing my grey suit and tie, not Saville Row, but the lads said it was o.k. I told them I would get a taxi back. On entering the lounge I was greeted by Alcadici who handed me a glass of grape juice. He asked if I had been here before I said I could not afford the prices, he laughed, and said he could get me a very good discount. Sid joined us and told me that they were all here. I knew a few of them but there were too many to mention but one was Fayed from Harrods. Sid told me they owned the Dorchester.

I told him I knew they were buying a lot of property and this was making prices go sky high. Sid asked me what I had in my grapefruit juice, when I told him nothing he came back with a glass of what I could only say was Vodka.

'That's better' I thought.

I asked Juma how things were at Watia, he told me a few days after I left they had a storm, the biggest one they had ever had. The pipes were all full and the manholes were as well and the pumps kicked in and filled the tanks and they had a million tons of water after five years without any, Juma thought it was marvellous.

'Allah must be with us' he said. I asked how his young pilots were getting on 'Don't ask' he said smiling.

'Did you manage to get those spares for our friend in Cuba' he asked.

I told him I had not had any luck so far and asked if he had been able to obtain them. He shook his head.

He told me that the only man that he thought could get them was Kossonggoi. Later that night I said my goodbyes and told them I hoped to see them again but I knew it was very doubtful that I would. I seemed to have lost all my energy, I was just going through the motions, it was a good job that I had some good workers around me. Bill was the one who had noticed the change in me, so I told him about Joyce and said that Shiplake would be my last job away from home. Phil had to go to Avenue Road as the fittings had arrived from Dolphin, silver taps for the bathrooms and the golden swans for the master bathroom. There were old fashioned brass types for the kitchen units in the centre of the kitchen. John had to go later as the chandeliers had arrived, the main one being for the stairway coming from the top floor which was bolted to the roof beams as it was very heavy. There was a small chandelier on the next floor and a bigger one on the next with a very large blossomed out chandelier on the ground floor in the hall entrance, it looked *splendid* as Sourfraki said. There were two beautiful ones in the lounge with another in the master room on the first floor, the rest were ordinary chandeliers on the top floor and basement. When these were done the men went back to Shiplake. The fibre plasterers had finished, Sourfraki had passed it and said he was very pleased so I paid the rest of the invoice. There was only the decor company now working and the carpet people. When they had finished and Sourfraki had ok'd the work I settled their invoices. That, as far as I was concerned was the end of the project. He had asked if Stephen the scouser who lived not too far away would stay also Alan, the part time gardener. They said they would and their salary would be paid by Emile or Sid.

I left to concentrated on Shiplake. Mr. Gordon came on site every day just for a few hours he was a godsend to me as I was doing my accounts. I had brought my touring caravan down and was using it as my office and I also slept there. A lady had called to ask if there was any temporary work like office or accountancy. She was in one of those little cottages as you entered Shiplake. She was just what I wanted, and I asked if she would call and see me. The next day she called, I said that my books needed to be typed out, checked and the totals from Avenue Road as this was completed and I had just started another account for Shiplake which she could look at afterwards. We agreed an hourly fee and off she went with all the necessary information including the cheque books. I told her to make the SU properties a separate account. Sourfraki would come to the site two or three times a week but didn't seem to be all that interested, he was more concerned about the furniture going into Avenue Road. He wanted to know if John could put another plug in for him and Colin to ease a few doors now the carpets were down. I told him that it would be no problem. He told me that a Mr. Henry an accountant, was coming the next week to go through the accounts with me and would I make sure that everything was in order. I couldn't help thinking it was all a bit late, I could have done with his help earlier. Shiplake was working fine, the men were all happy they had found a good local and began to know the people around.

Lady Grade lived a few doors away and came to see what we were doing. She was a very nice lady but she was annoyed with the tramps next door. I told her I was also annoyed and I also told her about putting my foot in it. She laughed, and said that had made her day. The top of the road which came down to Fairacres was blocked off, there was a footpath and at the end of the drive was a very large black and white Tudor type house, Vince Hill the singer lived there.

One night we went out in the motor boat as the lads had been able to start the engine. He came out shouting and waving his arms at us, we all waved back, and I thought he knew the lads so I waved as well. We would dock outside a pub we had come across in Henley and have a few drinks then we would go back to Fairacres about 10:30pm. One night we arrived back and found the police waiting for us, oh not a break in I thought. 'We've had a complaint that you are racing about in the motor boat, did you know there's a speed limit on the Thames?' the officer said.

'You're joking' I replied.

Danny said that we didn't know.

We were then told that there was a fine of £100 for going over ten miles an hour.

'Bloody hell, the lads in the rowing boats go faster than that, we've seen them going past here' I said.

'Yes but their boats don't make waves like a motor boat, the owner has complained that your waves have flooded his rose beds and went as high as to reach his front door' the policeman said.

I said 'We thought he was waving to us, we've talked to him many times and he's always been pleasant.'

'Well it's up to you lads, either pay the fine or go to court' he said.

'We will go to court and see him there, in a case like this you could have given us a warning coming from the Potteries, we've never heard of such laws.' I said.

When they had gone, I asked Phil who was driving, how fast we were going.

'About twenty with my foot down, it doesn't go any more.'

'Bloody twenty, let's just hope Vinny doesn't want any publicity and drops the charges, someone had better apologize.' I said.   We never heard anymore about the incident but the lads kept to under ten miles an hour after that and always gave Vinny a wave as they went past and later he started to wave back, laughing. Many years later he came to Jollies night club in Stoke on Trent and I wanted to talk to him about what had happened but never had the opportunity.

 Jean, the lady who was checking and typing my accounts had finished Avenue Road and SU and was now beginning Fairacres. I told her that everything was fine, especially as she had given me some photocopies. They became very useful for me later on. I paid her cash and thanked her and I said I would drop off the Fairacres invoices at a later date. Back at Avenue Road Mr. Henry was there, I gave him the accounts, and was feeling pretty pleased with myself as I was just under my budget price of £525,000. He was there all week also people from SU properties for which I was not responsible for, but paid, it came to £140.000.

I thought this would please Sourfraki, as Mr. Gordon told me the U.S. Embassy had offered three million for it and he had turned it down. The house prices were going higher by the month he was a lucky man, as money makes money not work I thought. There was nothing for me to do at Avenue Road, the lads had moved everything belonging to them, even the office desk and chairs and the old cooker and second hand T.V. The only time I went there was to pay Steve his wages and to pay Alan the Gardener, as I was still using the same bank at St. John's Wood. Mr. Henry said there was a meeting at 10:30. am at the flat in Kensington and he and myself would have to be there as there was something wrong with the accounts. He asked if Sourfraki had spoken to me. I told him I had not seen him for a couple of weeks. On the Thursday I made my way to the flat but was very late, as coming into London from Henley was a nightmare. I arrived at 11.10 and made my apologies to Sourfraki, Sid, Emile and Mr. Henry but they seemed very surprised to see me.

'I did not expect to see you here' said Sourfraki.

'Mr. Henry told me I was to come' I replied.

In the other room, the large lounge, were the usual Arabs.

'Roy, Mr. Kossenger said, what do you make of the accounts?'

I told him I was very pleased as my estimates were pretty close.

'But there is a discrepancy of £80,000 between you and Mr. Henry, how do you account for that?'

I pulled a copy of my accounts from my briefcase and handed it to them. I told them I had checked them and as far as I was concerned they were correct but I was not an accountant like Mr. Henry. I told them I would like to explain where I had gone wrong. Mr. Henry started to go through his papers and he told them that my accounts were correct but I had not entered a number of other cheques that he had there. There was also a cheque for £1,800 that had no receipt.

'Let us see them' they asked.

I saw Sourfraki getting very angry. Sid would not look at me and Emile looked like death.

One of the Arabs asked why was a cheque for £21,000 made out to Hamptons Mercedes Garage, Reading.

'I don't know, I've never seen it before and I certainly don't know the garage' I said.

They asked if Mr. Henry could shed some light on this and he said that the cheque was signed by E. Surfrundra.

'That is my car I bought, it should not be in the account, it is a mistake' he said.

'There is another one here for £8,000 signed by you, things must have got separated from my accounts' said Emile.

Mr. Henry was asked how many cheques he had signed, he told us there were seven, and four signed by S. Hewitt. Turning to me they asked if I had given them permission to sign cheques. I told them I was told by Mr. Hewitt I was the only one to sign cheques from that account.

Sourfraki began talking in Arabic, that gave him away as far as I was concerned. The discussions went on for about an hour. I was only interested in the £1,800 missing receipts. These were for tea, coffee, milk etc Steve had bought from the local shop for eighteen months plus a second hand desk and chairs for the office and a cooker and T.V. for the men who stayed in some night. These were the only things I did not have receipts for.

'I may have had the odd packet of cigarettes and a newspaper but that is all.' I said.

I asked if I was needed any more as I thought I should leave and they again started talking in Arabic, that was a sign they did not want me to hear. Mr. Kossenger thanked me and said I had nothing to fear. I walked into the other room where there was a large fellow that I took to be a bodyguard, he never got up even when I went down the stairs I did not wait for the lift. By the entrance doors there were two more men but they just opened the doors for me, this was the time I wished I had got Halami and Said with me I thought. I drove straight back to Fairacres stopping in Henley for a drink and something to eat but struggled as my stomach was turning over. I was expecting to be thanked but had practically been accused of theft. At Fairacres I told Bill what had happened and he was disgusted, he said he did not like Emile and that Danny had done a lot of work for him. He asked if I knew that his father was in jail, he was the Surfrundra who was exposed by David Frost for insurance fraud.

'That's what I want to talk about later.' I said.

I had more or less made up my mind to leave but I thought I would sleep on it.

At 6:00pm the men were all in the cottage getting ready to go out that night. As they were all there I decided to tell them all that had happened.

'The bloody crook, he came here in that sports car saying he had bought it but didn't mention that it came out of your budget.' said Colin.

'There is also a cheque made out for £8,000 and further more one made out to Danny Evans for £5,000, what was that for Danny?' I asked. The men went deadly silent.

'It was for supplying a kitchen unit for his mother in Reading and myself and John and Phil fitted it but it was in our own time we worked nights and a couple of weekends' said Danny.

'But did you know where the money came from?'I asked.

'No' he said.

John said that he only worked a couple of nights fixing extra lights and plugs which Danny had bought. Phil said the same, he just plumbed the sink in and he only had £50 and John had £100.

I told the lads I was thinking of leaving tomorrow and if they wished to carry on they would be working under Emile and Danny from then on. I stayed in my caravan that night. I had phoned my relation Graham who had a tow bar on his car and asked if he would come down in the morning and tow the caravan back to Silverdale where I kept it. The next morning about midday I went to the bank at St. John's Wood as usual and drew the wages for the men. I also asked why I had not had a statement. The young cashier went to ask the gentleman sitting behind her who looked at his computer.

They said they were sending one every quarter and it was going to Grange Securities in Jersey. I was asked if I wanted one to go to Avenue Road. I said no, as the property was more or less completed and we had started on the property in Henley. I went around to Avenue Road and paid Steve and Alan their wages and told them I was leaving that day and they would be working under Emile and Danny. They said they had not seen anybody for a couple of days and they wanted to know what was going on. I told them very little as I thought it was appropriate at the time. They said they were not doing any more work unless they knew what was happening but they said they had got my phone number and would be ringing me some time.

Back at Fairacres at about 2:30.pm the men were already packed for going home. Bill and a few of the others had their sleeping bags and said they were not coming back. I paid Bill and the others their wages with a little extra bonus but told Danny, John and Phil that Emile would pay them not me which they did not like one bit. Graham had arrived and he hooked up the caravan. I gave the car keys to Danny and drove off with Graham towing the caravan. I never heard from anyone again, only second-hand tales from Bill who still called around to my house and I enjoyed myself laying a few bricks with him.

Jordon / Israel -1984-1985

I knew this contract was trouble but decided to take it on because my old friend Alan Walsh was Project Manager and I had not seen him for years. My relationships with Arabs were not good, having had four years in Libya. It had been about eight months now since I left Soufraki. I had a phone call, it was from an M. Khalid who was the manager for Hal Habtoor in Jordan. He wanted me to join Alan in Amman on a monthly contract, which I liked, as Joyce was getting worse. So I joined Alan in the Ramada Hotel in Amman that was because foreigners could get a beer there. Alan was still drinking. We were booked in for the night so we talked of old times. Alan was downing three to my one. After a while I left him talking to some friends. I was tired.

Early next morning around 7:00am I went down for breakfast. Alan was there I really don't know how he did it! Two men picked us up, they were Alan's workers, one was his driver and cook Hamoud Fowzie the other was Fadia a JCB digger driver, the project was a 300 room hotel, eight storeys high built in the side of a mountain as it was in a valley called Zaqur Mien Hiem (valley of death as the psalm says). It is supposed to be the lowest place on Earth. You look up to the Dead Sea a mile away at the end of the valley and the sea is recognised to be the lowest. On the right was the river Jordan where John the Baptist baptised Jesus, high up on top were the ruins of Herod's Palace, where John had his head off, and further along on the left side was the cave where they found the Dead Sea Scrolls, it was an archaeologist's paradise.

The hotel was already constructed, supervised by my friend Giff who had left a couple of weeks before I arrived. He had worked here for two years, later I realised later he deserved a medal. My part was to oversee finishes and complete the outside areas, the roads were already in and tarmacced, just a few little areas to complete. The camping areas only needed the toilets to be glazed and tiled. The staff building was about 100 yards away – a square building comprising 16 flats that was constructed but nothing had been done inside. Also there was a supermarket with flats above.

Alan and I lived in a beautiful two bedroom bungalow that Giff had built two years earlier with a toilet and shower all plumbed in. The staff workers lived in trailers similar to those we had in Libya. The main workforce was about 60 Indians and 100 Pakistani's with a dozen Arabs who never did any work but sat around making che (tea). Their head man was named Knife and the rest were his sons or relations from the local village and to stop any aggravation they were given the job of security, and any light duties of which there were none they said. The management was Alan, myself, the two men who met us at the hotel, another man who drove the pick-up and dumper, and one who looked after the staff area and helped the cook. They were either Egyptian or Syrians. There was another engineer section they were PLO, spoke good English and I got on very well with them, especially Ali, a small young engineer. He had been here two years and was Giff's right hand man. One was in charge of the concrete plant making sure the Pakistanis mixed it correctly. Another was a Jordanian, Ader. He was supposed to see to the finishing of the staff quarters, but nothing was being done. Then I had it he was a lazy bastard, I didn't know whether he came under me or the PLO head man who never came out of his office to inspect the site and after 11:30pm Alan could not be found, anything I wanted to know would have to be between 6 and 11:30.pm.

Being 5 km down in the valley the heat was as bad as Libya, it was like breathing fire. The road down to us was an engineering masterpiece I don't know who constructed it but they were good, on one side of the road just in a gully there was a Land Rover I asked what it was doing there. Hamoud told me it was the first engineer and they went out one night for a drink in Amman, coming back they landed there. All four were found dead the next morning and it is Arab law not to touch the vehicle in fatal accidents, so whenever I saw a vehicle by the side of the road and I saw so many because you don't need a driving test to be able to drive I crossed my chest. I could see lorries coming down and thought I'm glad I'm not driving, when they got to the bottom they got their mats out and (we called it 'bums to the west') prayed. The Indians lived on the left side of the valley in shacks with tin roofs, the Pakistanis on the right more or less the same as the Indians, they never mixed but I noticed the Indians seemed to have all the foreman's positions. If I or Ali wanted something doing we had to tell them and they would give the orders. If it was a good job the Indians did it, if bad the poor Pakistanis. The English fair play was beginning to rise in me but Ali advised not to interfere, Giff had tried very hard but only made things worse as the Indians refused to work and the Pakistanis were afraid to carry on themselves so I took Ali's advice.

Down the middle of the valley aside of the road was a little stream but I was told when it rains all the water from as far as Amman comes down here and it turns into a torrid *river flash* as the Arabs called it, and you could hear it minutes before it reaches you. Fad was working in the stream making the sides wider and lifting gabions into position as the Pakistanis had filled them with stones. Gabions are wire mesh one metre square to form a base with a bottom the same mesh and when filled the mesh top would be wired on, Jab would position them up the sides as many as ten each side that made it ten metres high, I hoped when we had a flash it would be high enough.

Ader was beginning to work on the staff flats, perhaps because of me talking to him telling him to get his finger out has his was the only job behind schedule but no, I later heard that Queen Noor was coming down to look at the progress. Unknown to me she was one of the architects and took a great interest in the project. She was Huzziani's second wife an American.

'I hope she comes in the morning not afternoon,' I told Ali.

He laughed, 'mine's the same,' he said.

Alan told me that night Queen Noor was calling on site. 'She'll be here about 10:00 am.'

Thank God for that time I thought I hope she stays all day being mischievous.

She arrived about 10:30. Alan was already sweating, and Semon the PHO head was in a smart cream coloured suit, he looked much younger that I thought, as I had only seen him from a distance. I could see six black four-wheel-drive cars coming down the road, one flying the flag, that must be her, I thought.

Semon told Alan to stand at the front and Mr. Smith aside of you. 'I'll be next and Ali next to me, Ader would be with the others.'

He didn't like that, I felt sorry because she was Queen after all, out of the car she came in a tight white pair of slacks, a blue blouse and a large headscarf. Smiling, she came across to us, Hal Habtoor and M. Khalid were in white Arab dress wearing headdress with a colourful band.

'Mr Walsh, Mr Smith, the English engineers' as we were introduced. she smiled, shook hands and Habtoor carried on down the line.

'He remembers you Roy,' Alan said.

'Yes fancy that.' Feeling pleased with myself.

She went everywhere asking questions

'Could you push for the fittings? I can't wait to see them! Let me know when they arrive,' she said to us.

It was 12:30 now, and Alan was beginning to look very anxious, when we got back a table had been laid with snacks and cold fruit drinks which Hamoud had proudly put on.

'It's going to be beautiful down here looking right down to the Dead Sea,' she said.

We all nodded in agreement, she discussed the work with us all for about an hour, much to Alan's annoyance, she said her goodbyes, shaking hands again, she said she was sorry to have missed Mr. Giff's farewell, he had done an excellent job don't you think? 'Yes ma'am,' I replied.

Hal Habtoor and Mr. Khalid stayed on to have a talk with us, especially to Semon as he had to sign for payments and Khalid wanted a cheque, Habtoor put his arm around me gripping my hand and smiling.

'Hello sir,' I said, 'we were very sorry about the Ave Road project.'

' But it is *we* who owe you a debt of gratitude, not one word was spoken about you, and I am pleased to see you are getting on with your life, anything you want just ask Khalid, I've given him instructions to look after you.' he said smiling.

'Thank you and goodbye,' he said, Allah..... something in Arabic he continued.

All the time I'd spent with Arabs you'd think I would have picked up a bit of their lingo, but it's true everybody thinks English is easy to speak and I cannot understand why we are so backwards at learning other languages. My excuse is I was always too busy teaching them English.

Everything was moving well but Knife was annoying me, he even kept offering me a cup of che, to which I always answered, 'Bollocks.' It's a good job he didn't speak English.

'Alan I've been here a month I'd like to go home a few days.' I said. I thought he might be upset but he gave me a British Airways ticket and told me to buy a return when I was ready to come back, he said he would reimburse me, so Hamoud ran me to the airport and back I landed at home.

Joyce was about the same, no better, no worse, and still diligently taking her tablets. I told Joyce and the girls about Jordan. They were all interested which was unusual as they had not bothered before. They said they would like to come over and go to Jerusalem. I said I'd try but deep down I knew it was impossible, Joyce was not well enough to travel.

Karen my second eldest daughter who was married, was due to have a baby in about four months time. She said my eldest, Julie, who lived at Meir visited nearly every day and I had a feeling she knew about her mum's illness. After all she worked at the hospital as a clerk. The twins were doing well, Michelle was playing her violin well now, we went to the school concert and she played beautifully. Joyce cried and I had a lump in my throat. I never told Michelle how proud we were of her that night, I should have.

Jeremy at first was a problem he was of a smaller build than Michelle and no one would believe they were twins. I had been teaching him football and every Sunday if I was at home I'd take him to the local lads and dads football club run by the local well-known Roy Doug Brown. At first being the smallest he felt intimidated and would just stand there looking the part but doing nothing.

'Go and get the bloody ball' I kept shouting, sometimes I lost my voice.

'Good!' he would say.

After a couple of weeks Alan phoned.

'When was I returning? Nothing to worry about, he said, but Ali keeps asking.'

'I'll be back on Monday.' I replied.

Returning to Zaqura Mien Hiem it was as though I had never left, only Alan and Ali welcomed me, nobody else seemed to know I had been away. The next day there was an awful noise of shots being fired and Knife and the Arabs were running up the valley as fast as they could run, even the PLO were doing the same, only Ali stood by me as two helicopters landed on a plateau opposite the hotel and soldiers came running down shouting and waving their arms, firing into the sky.

'Israelis,' Ali said, 'stay where you are they will not shoot us but they will ask questions.'

An officer came to me and asked where Giff was, I told him he had completed his contract and I had replaced him.

'And your name?'

'Roy Smith,' I replied.

'Nationality?' he asked.

'English' I said.

'Okay that is good, but I see Ali from the PLO is still here.' he said.

'Yes, he is a very good engineer, he is helping me,' I said.

'Oh well, we like to know what's going on, we call in now and again, be careful don't trust these Arabs, not many will stand by you, they run like rabbits but watch your back at all times.' he said.

They jumped back in the helicopter.

'Bloody hell, Ali you never mentioned them.' I said.

'They call now and again the nosey bastards,' he replied.

Making my way to the bungalow, a four wheeled drive vehicle passed me, Fad who had stopped his machine for the day was walking back with me he said 'The visitors, they have already started to use the camping area and use the stream for cooking and cleaning.'

Alan greeted me, 'you've had a visit I hear.'

'Yes, you bastard, you never told me about them, I nearly shat myself!' I said, overstating it a little.

'Have a bloody Mary, it will calm you down,' he laughed.

I scowled at him, 'I thought this was a dry country' I said

'It is, but,' pointing to his nose, 'where there's a will ... and I have Hamoud twelve bottles of vodka, twelve bottles of gin, a crate of tomato juice for you, might I add and a couple of bottles of lime, sometimes I have a visit from air pilots who come and stay the night, they love this place, so I've got a couple of boxes of Heineken lager for them I hope you don't mind.'

'No why should I?' I replied.

'Because it's half your money, we are allowed expenses each month and that's where it goes, he laughed, guess where I got your air ticket from! Hamoud is a good cook and puts a good meal on every night, I end up eating Alan's sometimes, he isn't a good eater, guess why.'

The vanity units and showers, toilets and bidets had arrived so they were being fitted after the marble floor had been laid, the same was going on in the flats. I had given up on Alan and was pushing it.

The men seemed to appreciate that I was taking an interest in their work. I had to move Fad and the JCB down to the bottom where the camping site was situated.

We were just levelling some ground so that people could park cars when some men started to shout to us.

'There's a woman dead in the lagoon' they shouted.

The lagoon as they called it was where all the water accumulated and when it got to a certain level the pumps kicked in and pumped it into a stream where it naturally flowed into the Dead Sea. I walked over and looked at the body, 'she doesn't seem to have been there long' I thought.

'I bet it was those in that car the other night that passed us,' said Fad. 'I had better report it.'

'Yes, it's best,' I said. Fad said that we should tell Semon, he had a phone in his office and could call the police in the village, that is where he lived with his family and he knew the police there.

The police came down later and took the body away, they said she was Syrian and guessed that adultery would be involved.

'It was raining in Amman so we can expect it any time,' Alan told me, 'make sure Fad and the JCB are out of the water.'

This I did and moved the men to other work on the flats, which was on higher ground. Sure enough about an hour later there was a roar, it sounded just like the hurricane I heard in Cuba and then there was a wave of water ten foot high getting higher and noisier. Stone boulders were passing about six feet in diameter, being tossed as though they were pebbles, they kept coming down the valley, they were very close now to the top of the gabions, and they were ten metres high.

'We'll have to raise them,' said Semon, who had come out of his office and stood by us. 'It's a good job Giff built the staff's and your building up here.'

'Yes, but Giff knew about all this,' Alan replied.

The gabions stood the pressure, so there was only a minimum amount of damage. While checking the gabions I heard one of the Arabs shouting at one of the Pakistanis.

'What's all that about?' I asked Ali.

'Oh, they haven't made up any gabions for them, the Arabs have to fill four a day.'

'Four? I could do that myself before breakfast,' I said.

I went across to this particular Arab, I made it known to him that they should wire up their own gabionsThe Arabs all got up, looking at me with anger on their faces, if looks could kill I was a dead man. Then I did something that I knew was or could be fatal. I turned my back and started to walk away.

I felt a pain in my right side, there was shouting and an Arab and Ali were on top of me, others were gathering round I managed to get up and help Ali who was fighting, hitting out and kicking. I managed to down a couple and got hold of Knife around his neck, shouting 'stop'.

 When they heard Knife screaming they all stopped. By now a group of men had surrounded us, with that and me holding Knife they put their knives away, I slowly let go of Knife and quietly he and all the Arabs walked away up the valley collecting all the tents and equipment, that was the end of them I thought.

My side was covered in blood, I was looking at a gash about four inches long and Ali was holding his shoulder and had got blood on his face.

'Come on, we had better get this seen to.' I said to him.

Back at the bungalow, Alan and Semon had already been informed and told Fowzie to drive us up to the village where there was a PLO clinic, we had a few stitches, nothing to worry about, I'd had a tetanus injection six months before, but poor Ali had to have one.

'That was worse than the stitches' he moaned.

Getting back, Alan greeted me holding a rifle. 'You had better keep this, there will be trouble tonight,' It was a very old Royal Enfield 303 with a box of ammunition.

'Bloody hell, Alan it's a long time since I've fired a gun.' I said.

That night sure enough bangs were heard raining on the roofs of the trailers and the bungalow.

'That's what they do, give them about half an hour and they will stop throwing the stones from up there.' Alan pointed above, 'and then give them a few shots, I'm going to have a drink.'

'Do you want me to have a shot at them?' Fowzie offered. 'That thing,' pointing at the rifle, 'fires short, the sights want raising.'

'No, I'll have a go first.'

Bang, it fired, it was about twenty foot short of the top, you could hear the bullet in the rocks.

'I see Fowzie,' I said.

The next one went over the top somewhere but it must have annoyed someone as it started to rain rocks again. Taking cover I gave the rifle to Fowzie, I could tell he was dying to have a go. 'Giff taught me,' he said as he smiled.

Bang, he fired a few times and every one over the top, this seemed to have done the trick, no more stones, the Indians and Pakistanis all cheered and clapped.

Next morning Semon and the PLO engineers came, all smiling and behind them a mini bus with Knife and his crew, followed by the police.

'This fighting has got to stop,' Semon said. 'Someone was nearly shot.'

It must have been Fowzie I thought looking at him, I'm sure I saw a slight smile.

'The police have said to take this as a warning, and Knife has said as a peace offering they will make their own cages, is that acceptable Alan?'

'Yes, but from now on we require four cages in the morning and four in the afternoon, eight in total.'

Semon translated, the Arabs went mad, shouting and screaming at the police.

'How many do the others make?' said the police officer, who I had begun to recognise.

Semon looked at Alan who looked at me.

'Twenty,' I said. Ali looked surprised at first, then smiled.

The officer spoke to Knife, pointing to the Pakistanis I can only guess he was saying

'If they can do twenty, surely you,' pointing at the Arabs, 'can do eight?'

Their heads went down and the Knife said something about Allah and they started to walk down to the gabion site.

'Twenty, Mr. Roy' Ali said.

'Well how many do they do?'

'Twelve,' said Ali.

'Bloody hell, we had better put more men on it' I said laughing.

'That month's soon gone I'll be off on Friday.'

'And I'll go to the airport with you,' said Alan. 'I'm going to have a weekend in the Ramada with some of my old mates.'

Joyce managed to pick me up at the airport, how she drove I don't know, she looked very tired and had no colour in her face. Her hair was cut short she'd always had long black hair.

'Yes,' she said. 'My hair was coming out and thinning so I decided to have it like this.'

'It looked strange, but nice,' I said, lying.

To avoid cooking and cleaning I decided we would go out for meals, which the twins loved. I didn't want Joyce using any energy at all but she was adamant to still do things, she has always been so houseproud and her interior ideas were always admired by our friends. One neighbour annoyed her as she would go out and do or buy the same. The choices of furniture, decorations and colours at Avenue Road were all hers, Joyce's ideas were much admired by Janette, Soufraki's wife. Regent's Decor offered her a partnership with them, but she refused saying that as much as she enjoyed London home was in the Potteries.

Jeremy was playing football and doing very well, it was because of the coaching her and Michelle were giving him Joyce said.

'She doesn't shout at me,' Jeremy butted in. 'I've been selected Captain for the school.'

'Well, I'll come and see you then,' I said.

'You'd better not shout it's not allowed, parents will be asked to leave,' he said.

And so I watched quietly with the other parents, he was the smallest lad on the field.

'But by the far the best,' said Mr. Williams, the Sports Teacher, to me. 'I think you may have a sportsman here.'

After a couple of weeks I was flying back to the valley, in my mind was the feeling this cannot go on, but we had decided to carry on as usual for the twins sake, the two oldest girls knew how ill Mum was now.

The site was running well and everybody was pleased. Looking through the large lounge window you could see down the valley a beautiful view. On the right hand side was another large window, but only looking at the mountainside. Further along was a waterfall what if I could divert it to fall in front of this window? It would be another good view for visitors. I suggested it to Alan and he to Semon

A few days later Queen Noor came down again accompanied by two other cars. She walked around the site with two officials who had come with her plus Semon and Alan. Ali and I kept our distance in the hotel until Alan waved for us both to join them.

'The Queen thinks your idea is splendid, carry on with it.' Semon said

Oh dear I thought, it was only an idea, I've no way of knowing how to do it, I'd better get my thinking cap on.

'Any ideas? I said, looking at Ali.

'No,' he said.

'Well, I think if we get Fadi to make his way up there to the plateau and over to the water that flows over the edge, it's only a few inches deep and then we could excavate a trench from there to the front of the window for about thirty metres.

 I reckon then go back the way he came breaching the last metre where the water is flowing collecting as much rubble as he can and laying it on the edge of the top of the waterfall that should divert the water along the new trench.

Fadi agreed. 'The only problem is making a track up to it I may have to change my bucket on the front to a chisel it looks very rocky.' he said

'I told them to make a start straight away, if there were a lot of rocks all the men making gaibons could collect them and use them to fill in.'

It took about a week but Fadi did it. My heart was in my mouth sometimes seeing him getting higher and higher, if he ever slipped over the edge I shudder to think. As he was coming back he shouted for me to go to him. I was watching the water coming down forming a beautiful waterfall, and it could be seen from inside the hotel.

I climbed up to him. 'Great, a good job done, what's the matter Fadi?'

'Look what I've found' he said excitedly. 'I've only scratched about three hundred mil and look what's underneath.'

Right there was a beautiful mosaic floor.

'Keep clearing it, let's see how long it is.'

Which he did, it ended approximately four metres wide and six metres long, a beautiful, colourful mosaic floor, patterned with a large peacock and other little birds and flowers around it.

'We'll show it to the archaeologists at the weekend, it looks a good find, Fadi.' I said.

Later he shouted me again, near the bottom of the track he made was a wall, and you could tell it was man made the way the rocks were stacked carefully, Fadi made his way around until he found a door opening. The labourers started to clear inside, as some rubble had fallen in. Inside was a large stone bath big enough to hold six people with two troughs and all around stone like seats cut into the side of the mountain.

It looks like Roman baths from years ago for the soldiers, but I cannot understand the two troughs, they were for water but were at one end, I told the men to dig by hand and they came to a slab about twelve inches square, water was trickling out around the edges.

'It's loose,' they said. 'It slides up' and as they said it water flowed out, cold clear water along the trough to the bath and as they carried on they found another but this one was as black as the rock. Up on the plateau I had found that the water there got so hot you could not touch it and it had a horrible smell of sulphur, I was told this was volcanic from more than a thousand years ago. Sure enough, as the men lifted the second slab hot water ran out along the trough but it all ran out at the other end of the bath, so I told the men to excavate there and we found a stone like the other two but this was up. I asked them to clean it and drop it into position.

The bath soon filled, men were jumping in washing their legs and feet but being very careful not too much hot, the two slabs controlled the flow.

'Yet another thing of interest for the Archaeologists.' Fadi said.

When they arrived on Friday night and set up camp, the men walked down and took them to what we had found, I left them to it. Next morning Fowzie woke me for breakfast.

'I don't know what is going on, but there seem to be dozens of people down on the site with TV cameras, and the police are shouting and waving.'

'Oh it must be the bath,' I said. 'I'm keeping away.'

A police officer came knocking at the door, and asked Alan what he could do about it.

'They've been coming down here before I arrived,' Alan said.

'Well, I'm going to put a station at the top and stop people from coming down here unless they have a permit.'

'Good idea,' said Alan. 'Too many people will interfere with the work, we are behind schedule as it is.'

Queen Noor came down, she was all excited. 'It will be a wonderful attraction.' she said, 'and the water is marvellous all this from an idea the engineers came up with.'

'Yes,' said Alan who stood next to me. 'Keep your bloody ideas to yourself next time, the way things are going we'll be down this hole for years.'

I don't understand he's got a great life here, I thought.

A few days later we had the usual visit from the helicopter, the Israelis shooting and shouting, Knife and the Arabs running up the valley.

'Mr. Smith, there seems to have been a lot of excitement in the last few days,' the police officer had got to know me by now. 'What's it all about?'

I showed him around and he said the area was steeped in history, but he himself was more worried about the future. 'How about you, Mr Smith?' he asked

'I feel the same, but it's interesting, how on earth did they do these things years ago? that floor is a work of art.'

He agreed. 'Well everything is fine here, see you again Mr. Smith thank you.' and he offered his hand, funny I had not shaken his hand before.

While I had been down here I had been doing a lot of walking and at the same time trying to educate myself. The Dead Sea was salty because that is where supposedly Sodom and Gomorrah were turned into salt stone. Rumours abounded here, this was the West Bank, in the bible it was called 'The Wilderness' and I could see why, sitting on higher ground it looked awesome but very mysterious and weird in a way, there was something that made you think about religious things but I had lost my faith a long time ago, was that perhaps why Joyce was ill, was I being punished?.

I had been to Jerusalem and done all the tourist areas, it had done nothing for me, actually it made me feel worse, people trying to sell me leather sandals like Jesus wore, clothes merchants that made their own robes, they were all trying to sell you something. I saw Jericho, Jerash, Bethlehem, The Sea of Galilee Over the bridge was the British Army building called Allenby where you had to have a piece of paper with the Jewish Star stamped on it. This was instead of stamping your passport, as the Arabs wouldn't let you back in if you had a star in it.

A Professor from Amman and another Archaeologist said the baths we had uncovered were Roman, at the side would be their villa and the floor was a typical example of that period, there had been a landslide or even an earthquake, that had covered them up and we had uncovered them which he thanked us for.

Work was beginning to slow down as crowds of people were walking around. The police had been instructed to stop unauthorised vehicles, so they parked at the top and walked down, we tried to explain that people were the problem not vehicles.

'We will have to have orders changed,' said the guards.

Anyway I would be away on holiday in a few days so I didn't make an issue of it.

Fowzie ran me to the airport, shaking hands and saying, 'see you in a couple of weeks.'

But little did he know that was the last time I would see Jordan again.

Many months later Alan told me that the Israelis attacked the whole area and destroyed it completely, even the bungalow but before the attack the police and the helicopter gave them all one hour to leave the valley so no one was killed or injured. They claimed it was intended as a Recuperation Centre for the PLO and thinking about the PLO being involved made me think perhaps it was so.

The Wilderness

The wilderness is a god-forsaken place, and I can understand it being so in the Bible. I'd walked miles around it, getting lost many times and finding my way back by climbing to a higher point and looking around for my bearings. I got rather lucky in finding items of interest such as arrow heads which had grooves where they had been lashed on a shaft, or axe heads that had been lashed much the same way, all made out of flint sharp edges that were used for cutting the skins off animals, some were brilliantly shaped as hair combs. My collection was taken to the school in Clayton that my children attended, and as far as I know are still there.

One Sunday afternoon on one of my walks I had a feeling of someone watching me, but could not see anyone, it began to annoy me and no matter where I went I could not shake it off. Eventually making my way back to the site a man appeared, tall, thin, scraggy long dark hair, long nose with a coffee coloured face in a long greyish robe wearing sandals, his feet were dusty or dirty.

'Kief Halic Quis' I greeted him with what little Arabic I knew.

'Good afternoon,' he said in perfect English.

'Oh you speak English,' I replied.

'Yes, I speak many languages.'

'I wish I did, for me it's very difficult.'

'You are the engineer on the hotel complex, an Englishman?'

'Yes,' I nodded, 'and what do you do, are you an archaeologist?'

'No, I do many things in many places, Mosques, Synagogues, Churches like yours in Rome, are you a Christian?'

'No, I don't know what I am, I suppose you can call me a non-Christian.'

'The Christian religion has many faiths to justify themselves, but only one God,' he said.

I became aware that this man was a mullah or priest of some kind, and I felt uneasy.

'Can I offer you a drink or something to eat? We are not far from the site.' I told him.

'No, my friends' are waiting for something to eat, he pointed to the sky where I saw two birds (eagles I was told later)

'they always follow you, wherever you go, they think you are me, did you see them?'

'No but I certainly felt them.'

When I looked around he had gone, I asked about him and Abdel said it was the Rabbi who visits the valley from time to time. Weird.

Home and Work

Arriving at Manchester Julie my eldest daughter was waiting for me.

'Mother isn't very well so I decided to pick you up,' she said.

'Is Mum in hospital?' I asked.

'No, but I think she should be, you'll have to talk to her.'

I could see what Julie meant when I saw Joyce, she looked awful, no colour whatsoever. 'I think you need to have another transfusion.' I told her.

'Yes,' she replied, 'it's about due.'

She'd been having tranfusions every six weeks, so I rang the doctor who told me to take her in where she had the treatment, you could tell the difference in a matter of hours. Karen our second daughter had given birth to our first grandson, this also brightened Joyce up, she loved holding baby Daniel, for that is what he was christened.

I had decided not to go back to Jordan and when Alan phoned me I told him I would not be returning. He was very sorry but agreed that at times like this I should be at home. Bill, my friend who worked for me in London always called in to see how things were, or he would phone me. He lived in Brown Edge and was a self-employed builder, he would call saying, 'I've got a nice garden wall to build,' or 'a nice extension, do you feel like giving me a hand a few hours a day, whenever? I'll pick you up.' He knew I enjoyed laying a few bricks, it used to relax me, I now know what Winston Churchill meant when he said it relaxed him, and helped to get rid of the depressive feeling from time to time.

One day Bill called saying he had a contract bricklaying Mullers, in Market Drayton, and they were after a site manager. 'The job's yours if you want it.' he said.

'Bill I don't want to be tied down every day, I'm better just doing odd days with you or part-time.'

'Well there's a supervisor's position part-time that's yours if you want it.' he said.

'Okay' I replied. I worked there for nearly two years, in or around the Market Drayton area.

Joyce's transfusions were getting shorter, from six weeks to three.

Mr Ibbotson said 'Like chemo, transfusions will be of no use as time goes by the body will reject the treatment, her veins are getting brittle and are having difficulty carrying blood around.'

Injections were of no use as the liquid they injected just stayed there, the circulation was too weak to carry it around the body, tablets she swallowed stayed in her stomach no use at all. Ibbotson said he wanted her to have two days on his ward though I didn't understand why. It was for my benefit he told me later. On the ward were people we had met in his clinic, and we would get to know each other. When one was missing we feared the worst and as years went by it was only a matter of time when Joyce became the oldest. Ibbotson was letting me know what to expect from now on.

The lady across from Joyce who I recognised was only having suppositories and those weren't of any use her husband told me. She was having seizures that looked like fits to me, almost every half hour and one night she went into a coma, the next day she died.

I was in despair, choked, but glad that Joyce had not seen what had happened, later that day she whispered to me that she wanted to go home and not come back to the hospital again. Ibbotson looked at me and said 'yes'. In his eyes I seemed to read, 'you know what to expect now Mr. Smith.'

Our own doctor, Patel called at the house nearly every day giving her suppositories, also my sister-in-law, who was a case worker at the North Staffs Hospital called every day, and my cousin Debra who was a mid-wife, so there was never any problem of help.

One night there was a sudden movement, Joyce rearing up in bed with her teeth grinding. She was having a seizure, I held her close to me until she calmed down and then collapsed back on her bed, she never said anything, she just looked at me. I told her I loved her and stroked her forehead but got no response. The doctor called about 9:00am. I told her what had happened and then Joyce had another seizure, just the same as before.

'How long ago was the other?' asked Dr, Patel.

'Six hours,' I replied.

All that day I was counting the hours, she's very strong, people said, but I thought it was in her mind that she did not want to die and was going to put up a fight, to see her fighting on in terrible pain made me distraught. 'What can I do to help?' I asked her, but no answer came, just a look that seemed to go right through me.

That night the fits were every ten minutes, and still she would grind her teeth, that's enough I thought, we don't let animals live like this, I wanted to shout or scream or both, the last fit I held her tight, there was no teeth grinding she just went limp, I hugged her, as I knew I had lost her. How long I was there I don't know but I heard the doctor saying 'the children are upset Mr. Smith, they want you.' and he pulled me away.

The children were in the other bedroom crying, I put my arms around them and we cried together.

People were all very good, the undertakers came and took her away. Unknown to me Joyce had left the girls a list of what to do and they did everything to the letter. I remember seeing lots of friends at the funeral service but I was in a daze. The doctor gave me a couple of pills to take that morning and now I wish I had not taken them as I seemed to be smiling when I should have been crying and crying when I should have smiled. Thanking everybody seemed unreal, I don't recommend those pills to anyone.

Joyce was buried at Silverdale Cemetery about six graves away from her Father and Mother. The date is one I'll never forget -6th August 1987.

After a few days Bill called to see how I was, he told me to look after myself and the children. 'They need you more than ever now,' he said.

But as the weeks went by I realised it was me that wanted them to be near me. Gradually I began doing little bits and pieces around the house and garden, doing a little work now and again with Bill, but never for one minute did I ever forget my memories of Joyce. Looking after the twins was hard work, cleaning, cooking, shopping, paying bills, seeing to this and that makes you appreciate housewives. Glad when the children grow up and are able to look after themselves a little. I'm going to regret saying that in years to come.

As time went by, Karen had got divorced which upset us all, Jeremy had refused to play football again. Manchester City had given up on him, I think of all of us, he was taking it the hardest as he was mother's boy, nothing I could say or do was right, so I let him get on with it.

Bill called to say could I help him on another site, a large extension at Sadlers Pottery in Burslem, so I did a little part time work which got me out of the house, this lasted about a year and then Bill got a contract to build houses in Germany near Munich. 'No chance Bill,' I said when he asked me to go with him. 'I'm not well enough,' and although the children were now capable of looking after themselves I refused to go.

But after a week or so I was driving through Germany with Bill and his brother Steve. He had contracted some of the work to three men from the Potteries who had already been working in Germany as the wages were so good. I did all the driving as Bill and Steve could not get used to driving on the wrong side, it frightened them to death. 'You're driving on the wrong side' they used to shout when they weren't concentrating, at times I could not stop laughing.

The site was working well, Bill had got some good Potteries lads and good accommodation, a lovely, very clean guest house about fifteen minutes from the site, they call their guest houses 'pensions' which made Steve laugh, 'just the place for you two,' he said. 'We will go in the city tomorrow as there's no working on site, it's some religious day,' said Bill. So the next morning after breakfast we went down to the station it was beautifully clean, the train arrived, it was like our underground trains but travelled overland, it was fast and comfortable. Within minutes we were in the centre of Munich.

'What a beautiful place, that cathedral is magnificent and I'm beginning to wonder who won the war,' Bill said. 'let's have a drink it's 11 o'clock we can go in here.' He was pointing to a cafe. In the cafe was a bar with table and chairs the same as outside. 'We'll stand at the bar,' said Steve. 'What are you having Roy?'

'Coffee and Brandy.'

'And the same for me,' said Bill.

The lady behind the bar looked surprised. 'Are you English?' she asked.

'Yes' we all replied together.

'Ah I have good music for you, I love English, I have all records Beatles, Rolling Stones you name I have,' she said proudly.

Bill said, 'Have you Des O'Connor?'

'Yes' she shouted excitedly.

'Bloody hell' said Bill looking at me 'I only said it as a joke.'

I turned away doubled up in laughter and then I felt something against my leg. I turned back and there was Bill on the floor, his lips were blue I guessed straight away it was a heart attack. I shouted to the lady to phone for an ambulance and started to give him mouth to mouth, Steve joined me I told him to press on Bill's heart, counting four and release.

'Keep doing that,' I said to Steve. In a flashback I thought of my Medical Corp training, Ollie would be proud of me, it only seemed five minutes until the paramedics came and took over. They put the machines on his chest and something started to blip, I was so relieved, he's still with us, we did okay, I thought.

Steve was in shock, white as a ghost and kept repeating 'he's my brother.'

I was shattered, but kept listening to that machine blipping when I caught the paramedic's eye, 'blip okay?' I asked, he shook his head and pointed to the straight line. 'This your friend, the line, the blip is machine, sorry.'

'God, he's died,' I said in shock. 'I cannot believe it, having such a good time minutes before and all of a sudden this,' I said to Steve. He was crying uncontrollably, the paras had been trying for over half an hour when they stopped, they said sorry, but it was a massive heart attack, and he was probably dead before he hit on the floor. Later the Undertaker came and took Bill away, they spoke to the police who had arrived but stood outside keeping people away. The lady closed the cafe she was almost as upset as we were.

The police asked all their questions and I answered as Steve could not talk properly.

'Stay at you pension and we will let you know what arrangements have to be made' they said.

All the people at the pension were upset and were so sorry. Bill was only fifty years old. The police came and told us the Coroner would want to speak to us. After a couple of days they would release the body if the money had been paid to the Authorities' Undertaker and for the cost of transporting the body. Steve asked the Police if he could go home as he had phoned home and everyone was terribly upset, especially his son Robert who had answered the phone. I believe he had fainted when Steve had given him the awful news. 'But what could I do? Steve sobbed.

'Nothing' I said, 'I would have to do it if you hadn't, they had to be told.'

The Police said he could go but I would have to stay until the Coroner's meeting. I took Steve to the airport where he caught the Manchester flight. To make matters worse he had never flown before and was terrified, so I gave him a glass of brandy which seemed to help. The Coroner spoke good English, he said he was sorry, he told me what I already knew, that there was no question of foul play or neglect on the part of the Emergency services, this I agreed and signed, I also paid all costs and arranged for Bill to be flown to Manchester while I drove the vehicle back home.

By this time it was the weekend, the Potteries lads joined me saying they would have the weekend at home and return on Monday as I had asked them to finish the contract and they agreed.

I returned the vehicle at Bill's house, seeing his wife and children upset filled me with despair, I was going through the time again which I thought I was getting over. I attended the funeral and met all the old mates from the London Avenue Road job. It was nice to see them again and I would like Bill to think that we had all turned up and done him proud.

It took a long time for me to ease myself back into family life again, but slowly began doing things around the house and garden. Julie had bought a house in Meir and was happy. Karen had re-married and bought another house with Mark Holton, the Olympic hurdler. The twins and I quietly carried on at home, although Michelle was beginning to boss us around. Perhaps we needed it.

National service squad. Oliver Reed wins his first stripe, I am third from left middle row. Ollie is on the front row, barking!

Silverdale villagers.

CU?ALSE
Oficin Central
Oficios 170
Habana-Cuba   R 2-1388

Sr. Roy Smith.

Ave 19-A #21415 Rpto. Atabey.

Ingeniero.Mecanico. IMEXPAL.
        Exclusivamente. Diplotienda
Diplomercado.
        Vence.18-5-78

                            FIRMA

1976 Holland to Cuba. The only 'Hairy Arsed Bricklayer' to have the diplomatic pass, signed by the British Embassy.

Yours truly.

Some of the men in Libya.

Libya, with Ilami my interpreter and best friend. Notice the yellow baseball cap that was given to me by Castro. I took it everywhere.

At St Kitts and Nevis with Prince Phillip.

'Setting out' with some of the older students.

'The Class System'. Rich westerner's homes.

The poor homes.

Silverdale villagers at Walleys brickworks.

My apprenticeship at Keele - winning my mortar board.

Why VSO ?

One day while I was watching television there was a programme on where Jon Snow was talking about the VSO (voluntary service overseas). He had been one and spent his time in Africa, Fatima Whitbread, the javelin thrower was also a VSO but in an advertising group. This started me thinking of those wonderful couples working on that leper's clinic in Cuba who I helped and by accident found the missile bases. They had said that the Dutch and Canadian VSO had joined the British and they were desperate for volunteers, so I rang them.

'Yes please, they said, send your CV.'

I managed to put things down on paper as I had never needed a CV before. Julie who was in charge of management at the hospital helped me, 'not all that, Julie.' I kept saying. 'It's only a letter not a parcel' feeling very embarrassed.

A few days later I received a letter asking me if I would come to Head Office in Putney. It gave a date and time and said expenses would be paid, so off to Putney I went, travelling by train. Arriving at the reception desk I was told to have a seat and a coffee until someone came down to see me, this turned out to be one Andy Bevan.

'I'm the recruiting manager,' holding out his hand, shaking mine.

'Roy Smith' I said.

'Yes Roy, I've seen your CV and after reading it you are a VSO so don't think this is an interview for a position you already have. We just wanted to see you, show you around, and I'm here to answer any questions you might have.'

'Well, the first is my age, I'm nearly sixty, is that a problem?'

'No, we have many people in their seventies, the oldest is seventy eight, as long as you have some qualifications and you pass a medical, age does not apply, if you don't have the necessary qualifications we can sometimes help you with them, which is what we can discuss.'

'How long is it for?' I asked.

'That's up to you, we have six months, twelve month and two year contracts, we are desperate for medical doctors so if they can only do six months we are grateful, but of course we would prefer two years as that helps our recruitment staff.'

I asked if he could explain the financial side.

'We pay for all expenses such as today, your transport costs, your meals and if you wish to stay the night in your hotel. When you go on your project overseas the same applies, plus a monthly allowance which is decided by the government of that country. Say for instance you are going to teach in a school, you will have the same salary as the other local teachers, but we still pay for your accommodation because their salary is perhaps only twenty pounds per week, they can live on that but you are accustomed to Western living, hence that little bit extra.'

'So where and what do you have for me?' I said.

'Well, we want you on a few projects in Africa and Mongolia which you can start straight away, but the project which we are having difficulty in because the Government of that country keeps on pushing us is where we would like to go, but there is one snag, you need a teacher's certificate, this only takes a few weeks as you already have your qualifications and certificates, we will pay for all the costs, would you be interested?'

'Yes' I said.

'Good, I think getting this certificate may help you in later years if you should like to teach in this country, right,' he said, 'we'll have lunch we have a good canteen here and I'll show you around.'

I had a nice cottage pie with veg, dessert and a coffee, after that we started to look around. The library was very interesting, showing the places they work in, plus the many famous people who were once VSO's. Later a young girl came to us and asked if I could attend next Monday a course at Royles Hall, Manchester University. The course would be for four weeks, I said yes, but she asked would I need accommodation?

'No, I replied, Royles Hall is only forty minutes away, I would prefer to travel each day.' I told her. Right across the road was a place where I went for a medical which I passed with flying colours, according to the doctor. She too was a VSO.

The course was very interesting, there was about twenty eight people of all ages and all professions. As the days went by it got more difficult standing up in front of the group giving a lecture for twenty minutes talking about anything you wished, some refused and left, some tried and stopped well before time saying they could not carry on. I found it alright, only a few nerves but after a couple of weeks found it easy. Making a schedule before the lesson seemed to be difficult as I tended to stray from my schedule and the group who had copies would let me know. This turned into a nervous time as they would hiss and boo, it became a big joke which is precisely what the group teachers wanted.

By the end there were only twenty of us eight people had left some saying it was doing their heads in. At the end the head told us that we had all passed the preliminary course and would after a week's rest go to Oxford University of Further Education.

'That is where you will practice all the things you have learnt here, we do it this way as it costs a lot of money to send you to Oxford, and it must be worth it, as you know eight people have already left, just imagine them going and then leaving there it would have cost the VSO thousands of pounds, the VSO have not lost them but they will be offered alternative programmes, we can always find them some project.' The head said.

It was unreal, I was going to Oxford at my age, the children just stared in amazement and I was embarrassed. At Oxford a week later I met the other VSO's, there were eighteen, but two were missing, yes, it was the same as Royles but this time I accepted accommodation and it was only two weeks. It got pretty hard for me, the old brain started to object but I slowly pulled through, it was the old story, standing up at the front and talking for twenty minutes it was made more difficult because they gave you an object to talk about.

My object was a tin of Heinz Baked Beans and to make it worse there were a number of Oxford students making it quite a group, and if they didn't like it they joined in more vigorously than our own group shouting and booing. Please don't ask about the beans, how I got through it I don't know. I explained how to eat them, with what, where they came from, how they got in the tin, what the tin was made from and where the label paper came from, which was a Brazilian forest and how it was pulped into paper, I think you have the drift by now.

'We will let you know if you have passed,' we were told, thanking us all as we left.

A few days later a letter arrived from The VSO congratulating me on passing, and a list of projects and places I could choose, but underlined in red were the words, St.Kitts, Nevis in the West Indies, which is better known as the Caribbean, the letter was signed by Andy.

'So Andy, when do I go to Nevis?' I said when I rang him.

'Next week,' Andy replied laughing.

West Indies /St Kitts /Nevis

The West Indies was my first contract with the VSO (Voluntary Service Overseas) which I had joined after my wife had died and my children were capable of looking after themselves. Why had I joined?

Certainly not for the money because it was only food and accommodation with expense money, it was that I did not want to be in any more aggravating situations. Depression was beginning to set in, and I did not care if I lived or died. VSO sent me to Oxford College of Further Education where I received a teacher's certificate to teach at a Vocational Training College, this was only for six months as I had already got the necessary qualifications in my trade, bricklaying and building construction.

There were twenty eight on the course but only ten received the necessary certificate, it was not compulsory, and although some were very good at their particular trades, they were terrified at standing on the stage teaching, nerves I suppose.

After this we went on a survival course, the teacher was an eccentric man but I enjoyed it, I later found out he was Barnes Wallace's son, the man who invented the bouncing bomb in the war. I was offered a number of projects and decided on St Kitts, Nevis. Teaching construction at the local school sounded good to me.

There were twenty on the plane to Antigua where we began to separate, all taking smaller planes to the different islands.

I was booked on the St Kitts, Nevis flight with three others. Two lads got off at St Kitts while I and a young girl named Marlene carried on to Nevis.

We landed in a field, at the end was a brightly painted shack. 'Where have we come to?' I said to Marlene, laughing. A policeman asked us for our passports, giggling Marlene handed hers over while a large man with ginger hair and a big beard grabbed my hand and said with a strong Scottish accent,

'Quinton Henderson, VSO, welcome to Nevis I take it you are Roy Smith and you are Marlene De Sor.' He turned to her with his hand outstretched. 'I have a car waiting for you that will take us to your school where they have arranged everything plus your accommodation.'

'Are you teaching at the school?' I asked.

'No, I'm a bee-keeper they call me the bee man, there are lots of bees on this island and I have taught them to make hives and therefore extract the honey. I've been here four years and built up a very good co operative which is now in profit,' he said proudly.

At the local school we were introduced to the head, Mr. Williams and then to Mr. Neil who was my boss, he was in charge of the centre that was connected to the main school.

'Only two classrooms?' I said to him.

'Yes, that's where you come in, to build as you are teaching' He laughed. 'You'll be a demonstrating teacher, I am a carpenter by trade so I'll help and do the classroom work, the other is for domestic science for the girls mainly, but you'll find both sexes will join both. The teacher is Mrs. Walters, a VSO who has been here for twelve months and lives across the road in that block built bungalow, and that's where you will be staying until we get you fixed up with something of your own choice.'

An elderly lady came across to meet me. 'Smith,' she said. 'Pat Walters, VSO told me to expect you, did you have a good journey?'

'Yes, thank you.' I said.

'Has Mr. Neil told you that you can stay with me until you have found somewhere you like?'

'Yes, thank you,' I replied.

'Glad you've arrived, Mr. Neil has been doing too much and he gets no help from Mr. Williams, they're at loggerheads you see, Mr. Williams would like to be head of the centre as well as the main school. There are four hundred students and the ones that are failing academically are sent here to him, well I'm afraid that's about three hundred of them, maybe more, with only two classrooms, two teachers and two part timers it's been too much for him, but he'll not complain to Williams.'

Settling in at Pat's was no trouble, she had three bedrooms, and I could have the use of them if I wanted, there was a nice kitchen and lounge with a balcony all round the outside, she talked to me, telling me all about the people and the island.

Nevis was connected to St Kitts politically but not by land, there was a ferry twice a day, four times in the tourist months. It was only half a mile across if that, but with the currents being so strong it took about thirty minutes to Bassaterre the main town of St Kitts. Charleston was the main town on Nevis, the population on Nevis was around six thousand, twelve thousand on St Kitts, so the latter had most of the shout. Each island had its own Ministers and Premier, but the largest always had the upper hand. When Great Britain handed independence to the islands it made each larger island take a smaller one under its wing, this way there were so many called by two names as Trinidad and Tobago, Antigua and Bermuda and so on.

I said to Pat, 'coming from the airport I noticed some beautiful villas and then some terrible shacks, what's that all about?'

'Well, she said, 'the villas are the very wealthy people mainly British and American and the shacks are the locals, they do look awful I know, but one thing I can say for them they are very clean inside, people dress well and eat well and there's no starvation but the materials to build here very expensive and only a few are able to afford them. As you get to know the people and the island you will love it as much as me.'

At school much to Mr Neil's annoyance, Mr Williams introduced me to the school at assembly, the only time I had any connection with the main school was then and once a month at a teachers' meeting. Mr Neil refused to join either but insisted that we did. I had a number of tools, enough for about a dozen students, it was on my list to get more, one mixer sponsored by the Italian government, sand, cement and lime, a couple of wooden moulds to make concrete blocks which we did every day, this would take forever I thought, so more moulds were put on my list.

We started to lay concrete floors or bases to build the next classroom, after that we started to lay what blocks we had, I demonstrated how to build corners and to bond on top of one another and then put a string line from the existing building to the new corner we had built. This was where most students learned how to lay the blocks, and I watched to find the ones who were doing it correctly. Two boys and to my surprise one girl seemed to be the ones doing well. Mr Neil and a part time teacher named Prentice had made two more moulds so I was getting the blocks made more quickly. Mr Neil asked me if I would take two nights a week teaching adults, 5 o'clock to 8 o'clock if the light permitted it. I agreed. This helped me as they were much more capable and I suspected they had done it before. When the light faded we went inside one of the classrooms as they had electric lights, and worked on theory as this was what some wanted to learn. They could lay blocks and make them but did not know what materials they required and how much and how many, therefore when asked to give a quotation they struggled. This I found out was the same with the students, I had a word with Neil, some could not read or write or calculate simple sums. I had asked them if there are four blocks in a row and you want to build a wall six blocks high, how many do you need? Hundreds, some said, very few answered twenty four, and when that had been accepted I asked how much would it cost if they were six dollars each? Just a handful answered correctly, one hundred and forty four dollars.

'Go and tell Mr Williams what you've just told me.'

'Be careful, Roy,' Pat whispered to me.

Yes, I thought, Neil should be telling him.

One Sunday morning as I was walking around the island which I liked to do, a man shouted me from a lovely building, not a villa but it looked a nice place, it was Mr Williams.

'This is my house,' he said proudly.

We sat on his veranda and his wife brought us a fruit drink, we got talking, and after a while I said. 'I would like it better if you and Neil were friends.'

'Well, we were at one time, we both went to college in Edinburgh, but we both applied for Head at the school and I got it, that caused the problem, Neil, to his credit, raised the money for the centre to be built but when it was joined to the school he objected. I was in agreement because the children could just walk across, not too far to travel, that honestly was my only thought, Neil thought I wanted to take control of his project but honestly it never entered my head. The other thing is and I must agree with him that the students you send to us cannot read or write and have no knowledge of maths or very little.'

'Yes, I plead guilty but think about this Mr Smith, if they were good at the things you mention I would not send them to you, I would gladly push them in the academic stream, I even keep some children behind if they only show a little common sense and I wonder sometimes am I doing them a favour or would they be better with you? You are doing a wonderful job, I don't think you know how much you are appreciated especially for the adult classes, there is plenty of work here in the construction trade, the wealthy people are always wanting some building or extension.'

I thanked him and his wife for the drink and hospitality, the experience had confirmed to me that it's best to know both sides of the argument before giving opinions.

A lady was always calling into the school, she seemed to be bringing things and I could see that she was interested in what we were building, she always spoke to Pat. One day I asked who she was.

'Oh, she's one of the Cadbury family, Margaret Cadbury, she's married to the heir of Schweppes the drinks people, and they live in one of those villas aside of the mountain, she's invited all of the VSO's to a barbeque on Saturday, it will be good food and drink and will be good to meet some friends.'

I spotted Marlene, 'hi Marlene' I said.

'Roy' she replied as she kissed me on the cheek, she was in a beautiful dress, she looked lovely.

'I've been hearing lots about you, I've been working in the Government Finance Office and I'm staying in a small flat belonging to Nigel, let me introduce you.' which she did.

Just then the Bee Man joined us, he always looked scruffy with his bag strapped on his back.

'Take that off,' Marlene said, he did with a smile.

'My Roy, we are with the money people now, that's Nigel Fraser from the House of Fraser shops in the UK.'

'Never heard of them' I said laughing.

Margaret was a great hostess, but did we not meet her husband as he was in the States, the food and drink was great and we from the VSO made sure nothing was left at night.

'I'm very pleased you have enjoyed yourselves,' she said.

'Not as pleased as we are being invited, thank you,' I laughed, and kissed her on both cheeks, everybody does that I said to myself as I was not used to it.

The school at last had another classroom, as we had put the galvanised roof on, Mr Neil decided to turn it into a carpenter's workshop helping to make furniture or anything to sell, we needed finance for materials and equipment, we also got a new woodwork teacher, his name was Williams but was no relation to the head. I was busy carrying on connecting another floor base ready to build the next classroom making blocks and teaching the adults at night. One man named Tony was building a bungalow in the next village called Bath, he only had a little painting and tiling left to do and he said if I would do it I could rent it at a cheap rate. He had got a contract on the next island, Tortola, and would be away a couple of years, so that is how I came to live there for eighteen months as I extended my VSO contract another six months.

Although there was more work than he first said, it was a good move, Pat didn't seem to mind, but people had begun to put two and two together and make five, if you understand my meaning. Unbeknown to me, the people had

had a meeting about whether to accept the white man in the village, no whites had ever lived in Bath, some said. But he teaches our children, others said, so they voted and I won. I was told this later on a very sad occasion when Mr Neil died suddenly, they said it was a blood clot. When Mr Neil died it was so sudden that we could not believe it, there had been no illness. Eventually it sunk in and the whole island was in mourning because it was his vision to start the VTC for children who had failed their exams.

'At least we help them learn a trade' he used to say.

He also managed to get the finance to start it and so he was elected to be the head. His wife and mother attended, and my adult evening students, the women on the island, in my opinion were the bedrock ground on which we built. To get things done it was usually the women to do it, when Mr Neil died they wanted to say thank you to everybody, they knew what to say but did not know how to write it down, so that night with the other adults we made it into a lesson. For people who had never been to school in their lives before I was amazed at their enthusiasm, Mr Neil's wife, Iona was in her fifties and his mother Glendora in her seventies and this what they eventually wanted me to write.

Perhaps you sang a favourite song

Or sat quietly in a chair

Perhaps you sent a funeral spray

If so, we saw it there

Perhaps you spoke the kindest words

As any friend could say

Perhaps you were not there at all

Just thought of us that day

Whatever you did

To console our hearts

We thank you sincerely

For your special part.

The Premier of the island Mr Vance Emery who funnily enough had lived in Meir in the Potteries for a number of years, asked me to take over control of the centre for a short time until they had a meeting on what to do. I said okay, but VSO had heard and advised me not to take control, we were to help, not to take over. This was agreed and I told Mr Williams that I would supervise but if it came down to being in charge, he was. This he was pleased with, and the only time he interfered was always to help.

He gave us the next classroom to ours and I turned it into an air-conditioned room to take ten computers that had been sponsored by an American living on the island. Rumours said, it was Bill Gates, I never saw him but sometimes I saw a private jet or a helicopter arriving at the airport. There was just one problem there was no teacher who could teach the students to use computers, I didn't know, I couldn't type never mind compute.

At last we got a young girl from the college over on St Kitts and a being a local she had relations on the island so accommodation was no problem.

'We've got another barbeque this weekend, Margaret and Roger Henderson, no relation to the Bee Man' Pat said laughing. 'He is a QC to the Royal Family and lives in that beautiful green and cream villa near to the Mosley's house.'

'Yes, I know the one,' the Bee Man had pointed it out. 'Mosley's son lives there.'

'Now can you remember his Father? He was a fascist when the war was on.'

'Yes, I vaguely remember him,' I replied.

'He's a miserable old bastard, never joins in with anybody and has not bought one jar of honey,' said Quinton.

'Seriously?' I laughed.

'I never saw him, but when he died I joined the other British people just showing the flag

The Henderson's were a very likable family, not at all like I imagined, Judge Jeffries comes to mind, and the food and drink was more than welcome, all the same people as were at the Cadbury's barbeque and it gave me the opportunity to speak to some new friends. One was named Bob, an old fellow with a long grey moustache, he was in charge of the generators that supplied the electricity and when it went off people would say, 'come on Bob, what's up?'

'So you are the Bob I hear of so often?' I said laughing.

'Yes, and you are the new teacher, I saw you at Mr Neil's funeral but I didn't get to speak to you, some of my workers go to your evening classes, it's great, and a big help to the locals.'

'Thank you,' I said. 'How did you come to be here? I am with the VSO.'

'Yes,' he said, 'same as Pat and Marlene, I come through ODA (Overseas Development Agency), the only difference is I get a very good salary from the agency, plus accommodation, it's who you know, not what you know,' he said, touching his nose.

Another couple I met were David and Nancy, they were ex VSO from Canada and afterwards decided to stay, they had a beautiful villa half way up the mountain, in Nevis, overlooking the bay. David was a historian, and showed tourists around the island, visiting the sugar plantations and showing how the slaves lived, how they made their rum, and the trees that the slaves grew their food on. They called them bread fruit trees and now they will not touch it. I did though, I found it sweet and tasty, but if any of the locals saw me they would point towards me and laugh. Nancy had a very good position as receptionist at the luxury Four Seasons Hotel, she would always tell me if there was anyone important there, in case I wanted to invite them round the school and perhaps seek a donation, people like Sylvester Stallone, the Rocky and Rambo star, or Arnold Schwarzenegger who came quite often for a game of golf, they did not come to the school much to the disappointment of the students, but they asked me if there was anything they could do to help the school.

'Yes, we are always desperate for chairs.' I would say.

A few weeks later we received one hundred chairs in a container, Lionel Richie, the singer called at the school to give a lesson in music, but he seemed more interested in what I was teaching, getting the students to lay concrete blocks and erect corners, levelling and plumbing them. I used to go round checking them, saying if they were not level or plumb, kick the bottom in or out, and to my surprise that was the theme of a song he and the student sang, 'kick the bottom in or out.' Many more wealthy people helped the school, too many to name, but I thank them all.

There was a very exclusive hotel called Montpelier, owned by a lady named Celia and her husband. Celia was a relation to royalty, so the rumour went and she called from time to time at the school, she too was interested in the vocation training centre, saying this was what was really wanted as a lot of youths were out of work and were getting troublesome. 'But at last you are helping to give them a trade.'

Marlene also knew her, and told me everybody had a nickname for her: Squeaky. She did have a squeaky voice but I never called her by that name and I never heard anyone else. Mr Prentice's wife worked for her in the reception office and through her I got invited for tea or coffee.

One day, through Prentice I got an invitation to a dinner evening with Celia, must wear a tie it said, funny I thought, but I turned up and sat at a table with the Henderson's and Bob.

'What's all this about Bob? I asked.

'You'll see, look over there in the corner.'

To my amazement, there sat Princess Diana and her two boys. After dinner Celia was introducing them to all the guests, lastly they stopped at our table, she introduced me to Diana as a VSO teacher at the new VT Centre.

'Oh yes I've heard a lot about VSO but you are the first I have spoken to, Celia has told me what a good job you are doing, I especially liked your safety lesson.' We shook hands. 'I do admire what you are doing,' she said.

'Thank you,' I replied and they left the room, the boys were laughing, my 'safety lesson' that Celia had told her about was something I used when I had a troublesome student, I used to tell them to wear a steel safety helmet and boots, this is in case anything falls off the scaffold and hits you on the head, or on your toes. Picking up a piece of 2" x 3" timber about two foot long I gave them a smack on the head, not too hard but enough to make them shudder, this usually stopped them from causing trouble if they saw me getting the safety helmet out.

When Diana said she admired my work I felt a lump in my throat, but instead of feeling delighted I became depressed, thinking but *I'm only a hairy arsed bricklayer from the Potteries*. Like many times in my life I became homesick but after a few days I was able to contain my feelings and carry on teaching. My brother Barry in Australia who had emigrated thirty years ago and never returned even for a holiday, said he suffered exactly in the same way, and to get over it they have what is called 'going walkabout.'

The school's next unit was ready and after talking it over with Mr Williams, we decided to have an auto-mechanics class because there was a shortage of mechanics on the island. He had trouble getting a teacher but after a while managed to get one on a part time basis and with the odd lesson from me we managed. I had bought an old banger from Mr Prentice who had let it go to rust as he did not have the money for repairs. This would be a good way of getting the lads to repair it, with the idea that when they got it going I would teach them to drive it. That did the trick it even got the academics joining in.

Mr Neil's old room I had turned into an electrician's classroom as requested by Mr Williams again because of the shortage of electricians, but none were forthcoming to teach, they were earning far more money privately, so VSO sent a teacher, Andrew Knowles, who was a University graduate with a knowledge of electrics. The subject did not go down very well with the usual students, they found it too difficult. Mr. Williams sent some of the academics down twice a week, I had asked Andrew if he could slowly demonstrate the basics as a private electrician had offered to take a couple of lads on, teaching them the practical side, Andrew seemed to be having a difficult time.

'But they have difficulty reading and writing,' he would complain.

I thought, he'll not be here long, and about six months later he left, VSO found him another position more to his liking on the island of St Vincent, luckily enough, private electrician Joseph had seen the advantage of having help and decided to teach two days a week. We turned the other three days over to an ex-student, Mr Morton who was an architect and would give drawing classes. The last unit was soon ready as it had an open front, this I wanted for myself, with all the building completed I required a place to teach them and show them how to build little corners and walls.

Celebrations were being prepared for the anniversary of Independence Day, Prince Philip was to commemorate the occasion. On the day the royal yacht arrived, it had to dock outside of the pier as the sea was not deep enough, so a large boat brought the Prince to the pier where he walked through the crowds to the cricket grounds pavilion. There on the field were all the children and staff with me in the middle, Marlene and the other VSO's were holding up a banner saying 'Welcome from the VSO.'

The morning he spent on Nevis, and the afternoon and night on St Kitts, where he held a barbeque and all the VSO had invitations, we all caught the ferry across and all looking very smart in our suits and dresses, even Quinton the Bee Man was wearing a brown suit and a tie. I'd never seen him dressed like this before.

'And you never will again,' he groaned.

The barbeque was in the governor's grounds, it was a beautiful afternoon, there were plenty of drinks and food, and it was much appreciated. When the Duke came across to meet us which he was doing to all who were present, he came to me first as I was asked to introduce the others.

'Did I see you over on Nevis this morning?' he greeted me, shaking hands.

'Yes sir' I said.

'I couldn't miss you, could I?' he laughed.

I was the only white man in the middle of four hundred coloured students, but he didn't say it.

As I introduced them all, he was surprised to hear Quinton telling him about looking after the bees.

'We have quite a number of hives at Balmoral, the honey is one of my favourites.'

'Yes, I know sir, that's where I learned my trade,' he told the surprised Duke.

'Well I never, splendid, I've always wanted to meet.'

'Well you are our Patron,' said Marlene, interrupting,

'Yes, but it's the first time I've been to the front line,' he smiled.

'What do you find you miss when working overseas?' he asked me.

I was surprised and not ready for questions, 'well,' stuttering for a reply, 'a pint of beer,' I managed to say. Someone else said a pork pie, and pickles said another, laughing, he moved on to the next group of people.

Later that afternoon one of his officers joined us and told us that we were invited to the Royal Yacht for cocktails and to see the retreat later that night.

Arriving at the gangway with the Premier and other dignitaries we showed our VSO identity and were escorted to the cocktail lounge. It was a wonderful sight, everything highly polished especially the brasses. I don't understand how they can call this a yacht, I was thinking when the officer who had invited us came and welcomed us saying he had a surprise for us, he waved to a very smart waiter dressed in white who came over to us with a long tray of pints of beer, another followed with a tray of pork pies cut in half and a dish of pickles. We all laughed and thanked him.

'Don't thank me,' he said, smiling as he left us.

We did not speak to the Prince, but we caught his eye, he was smiling at us, he was with the top brass, Quinton said.

Later we all went outside and looked down on the quayside, there, was the Royal Marines Band playing The Retreat, I had no idea what this was, but not wanting people to know my ignorance I never asked. The band played and marched up and down the quayside, it brought the hairs on my back to stand up, it really was magnificent. There were a lot of Americans watching and they were astonished at the order of marching as well as playing at the same time. It made you feel proud to be British, and that's saying something for me.

The ferry had been specially laid on for all of the dignitaries, so we joined them and landed in Nevis about 2 o'clock in the morning, a brilliant day was had by all. I had been on the island twelve months and was due a month's leave, which I took and returned home to my family, they were fine and I don't think they had missed me. I felt a little sad, but it's good that children should get on with their own lives, I thought.

Back on my way to Nevis, waiting for a smaller plane at Antigua, I got talking to a couple who were waiting for the same, they were having a few days holiday and staying at the Golden Rock Plantation which was run by Pam Barry. Her ancestors were the Barry's that served Nelson on his ships, one being a captain of the fleet, he was also the best man when Nelson married Fanny Woolward at the local church in Nevis. It is a tourist point where you can see their signatures in the marriage books. For his service Barry was given the plantation and grounds surrounding it, and over the years it had turned into a museum for tourists, also an exclusive hotel with swimming pool et cetera.

One day, Pat the VSO domestic teacher had invited a few VSO's to a meal at the Golden Rock, it was her birthday, Quinton said it was her sixty –fifth but nobody knew for sure and we were too polite to ask. As we sat down Pam introduced us to the people on the other table, I recognised the couple on the plane from Antigua. There was also Mr and Mrs James Michener, who had written a book about the Carribean, he was the author, who I remember wrote the original story on which South Pacific my favourite musical was based.

'Hi, we meet again,' he said in his strong American accent.

I wish I could write like him, I thought.

We had a lovely night and I was enjoying myself feeling the best I had felt for a number of years.

The centre was running smoothly, there were eight classes that were going great guns, and to everybody's satisfaction except I noticed at the monthly teacher's meeting a little envy creeping in. Perhaps we were going too well, and the academics were getting jealous. I thought I would take a slight step back and allow the local teachers to take hold of the reins a little more, I had convinced Mr Black the builder who had started the centre with Mr Neil to teach for two days. He had stopped because he had a contract to build a beautiful villa for an English couple who had won a large amount of money on Littlewoods pools, now that was finished he could spare the time, this helped me to have a little time for myself.

My daughter Michelle came over for the holidays with her boyfriend Nick, they had a wonderful time and with the old banger going again I was able to take them around the island, some days I would drop them off at the Four Seasons and Nancy used to look after them, they thought they were millionaires staying there with all the wealthy clients. After school I would pick them up, sometimes I had a paddle along the beautiful beach, but never swam again after the Cuban incident. They said there were no sharks, but there were, I caught the fishermen cutting off their heads and fins, saying they were dolphins with a smile on their faces. 'We're not to catch these,' they would say.

A friend of Marlene's came to the school one morning and went into Pat's class. I asked if she was well and how was Marlene but she did not answer me, she worked with her in the government office. Later Pat came to me and asked if I could drive her to Marlene's as she had been attacked and assaulted. When we got to the lodge where she lived, Pat walked in and I followed with her friend, she looked terrible and cried incessantly, all her things were already packed and she asked Pat if she could go and stay with her.

'Certainly,' she said, and asked me to load the cases in my car. We drove off and arrived at Pat's. I unloaded and then I left saying 'If you want any more help just come across to the school.'

'I think she only wants to talk to you.' Pat said. To me, it looked more serious than assault, but I would wait until Pat could tell me what had happened. The next morning Pat told me that Marlene had been sexually assaulted and they had been to the lady doctor at the hospital. Marlene didn't want to take it any further, 'So that was that' Pat said to me, I told her to be very careful.

'She was living it up with these money people and there would be a price to pay.' Pat said.

I nodded in agreement, she was doing the exact opposite to what the VSO stands for, this is one of the reasons I refused to get a higher position, we were there to help and share our skills.

At the end of term, the students played the staff in a cricket match, and of course all the village turned up and made a kind of carnival out of the occasion. I was down as number four batsman and considered myself a fair bat, so I started very slowly, picking a few runs here and there, the boys were bowling faster and faster.

'Get the white man out, bowl faster, give him a few bouncers the white men don't like it.' they shouted. A bouncer did come, and hit me right in the mouth, splitting my lip and breaking one of my front teeth in half and loosening the other. I was off to the clinic for a couple of stitches, but I would have to go and see the local dentist as they did not have one at the clinic. I had heard about the local dentist, they called him the witch doctor, and when I went into his shack to see him and saw his equipment I froze.

'I've got better in my garden shed.' I cried. 'No way, I'm off.'

I phoned Head Office on St Lucia.

'Fly over tomorrow morning, we have a VSO dentist here.' was the reply.

And so I did, flying from one island to another seemed to be the norm, they called the plane the island hopper, which seemed to fly whenever called if you didn't call it would just fly over to the next island.

The dentists were two Canadians, they were brilliant, they had to take the other half of my broken tooth out and the second tooth because it had broken at the root, they took impressions and told me to call back the next afternoon.

Nick Burn, my VSO director, had arranged for me to stay the night and he took me round St Lucia. It was much bigger than Nevis with more hotels and activities, the large cruise ships seemed to come right into the middle of Castries, which was their main town.

The next day the dentists fitted my dentures with a little adjusting here and there until they were perfect, and advised me to pack in playing cricket. Back on Nevis everyone was impressed with my new two front teeth and I found it a good ploy to take them out when some students (especially the girls) were acting up. They had not seen dentures before and it frightened some of them to death.

Pat told me Marlene had gone to live with Bob. 'She'll never learn, she finds it too quiet living with me.'

I was not concerned as I knew Bob could be relied on, and in any case he had a lady friend living with him, he had a four bedroomed bungalow, so there was plenty of room plus a car which Marlene enjoyed riding about the island in, as Bob allowed her to drive when he did not need it. Bob had a new ODA on the island named Euan Jones, he was doing a surveyor's report for the government and I became very friendly with him. He liked sport, especially football and whenever he saw me doing a little coaching with the students he would join in, he liked having barbeques and always invited us VSO's. He lived in one of those beautiful villas half way up Nevis with all the trees around and a balcony surrounding the villa it always reminded me of Tarzan's house in the films.

Why I have mentioned him is because I've just seen him on television, I think he is the first Welsh Minister, or is going to be, I'll have to try and get in touch with him sometime. He must have like Bob, been on a good salary as there was plenty of food and drink, this I was envious of, they were very politically conservative and me being a socialist I was working for a pittance, and to rub salt in the wound their boss was Clare Short, a bigger socialist then me, well it takes all sorts, I thought.

The school was quietly carrying on as normal until one day a group of older students were being familiar with a young American teacher and began touching her breasts and picking her skirt up. To my astonishment the other teachers did nothing about it, I could see she was distressed and although it was nothing to do with me or VTC I ran across and pushed some of the students away. I was throwing punches as they turned on me, one lad came at me with a piece of wood hitting me on my arms and shoulders, this boy I paid more attention to since with the piece of wood he was the most dangerous. Eventually the others ran away but I kept hold of the one with the wood.

Two things came to light while I was looking in the boys eyes, I could tell something was wrong, his eyes were glazed and his face was sort of twisted, the other was that I was covered in blood, I noticed his piece of wood had a nail protruding out at the bottom and it was this cutting into my arms and shoulders that had caused the bleeding. At least one male teacher out of the gutless staff-room came and helped me, we managed to get hold of one arm each and take him to the headmaster.

I left thinking they would deal with him but as I was walking back to VTC he came past me running like the devil out of school. No teacher, no headmaster was in sight, I thought, why bother Roy, and I took no notice.

Pat came running to me and seeing the blood she said, 'go to the hospital, you need stitches.'

So off I drove and was told by the nurse that there was no need for stitches as they were more like punctures not cuts, but she gave me a Tetanus jab.

Later I was told that the American teacher had left the island and told Pat to thank me for my help. The boys were all expelled, the leader of the gang was a minister's son and was in hospital, charges were to be made, but they never were, it came to my attention that he was a drug addict. Now I'm pretty good at noticing things, but never in a million years did I suspect drugs I'm afraid it was getting onto the islands the same as anywhere else.

'It has been passing through the islands on the way to the US and Europe, but some have been dropping off on the islands,' said the Premier, Vance Emery, when he came to give a talk in the staff-room. What use is that I thought, when it's your own ministers' son? It's them you should be talking to.

The last year I had seen a change in the young people and I came to the conclusion it was because of money flooding the island, sponsoring baseball, netball etc. They were becoming greedy and their parents were struggling to control them, the same as the teachers. The groundsman at the cricket ground, Mr Paris, who I always sat beside when watching a game told me, 'in a few years time West Indies cricket will be finished.'

'Never,' I said.

'Yes, Mr Smith, there are no boys coming through, they're all going to the States and Canada to play football and basketball, that's where all the money is,' he said sadly.

His prediction was true, the West Indies cricket team was now bottom of the league, after being the greatest team in many people's eyes.

I had the pleasure of attending a test match in Antigua as the English team was visiting, I said pleasure, which was not quite true as on the two days I attended Brian Lara was at the wicket and he broke all records, he scored 375 runs, beating Garry Sobers' world record of 365. At lunch time I managed to walk into the VIP room, I must have looked like someone important as nobody stopped me, and there were all the famous cricketers, too many to mention but one man caught my eye, Sir Garfield Sobers as he was named now. If I could only get closer to him maybe I could have a word with him. Gradually I managed to join his crowd and when he said he was delighted that Lara has broken his record I interrupted by saying, 'as an English supporter, I was not all that pleased.'

He looked at me and said, 'well, I can understand that, but you will always remember this day because it will be in cricket history and you will be able to say, I was there.'

'Yes, like I can say I used to watch you many times playing for Norton, a little village in the Potteries.'

He looked at me in amazement, 'I thought I recognised that accent, the same as my friend Tommy Talbot, did you know him?' he asked.

'Not to talk to, I said, but I was delighted that he brought such great players like you into our league.'

'Thank you, I have a lot of good friends in the Potteries and always look to see how Stoke football team are doing.' Slowly I drifted away, thinking don't push your luck, as quite a few people began to notice me. Yes, I would have loved to have said I'm a hairy arsed bricklayer from the Potteries.

On Monday morning back at school there was a notice on the staff board showing a rota of teachers to take the morning assembly, and it included teachers from the VTC. This caused commotion between us, we had never been included before.

'Was this where Mr Williams was showing his authority over us?' they asked.

I refused, as it was really a religious ceremony and I did not go to Church, I said that I would be willing to take assembly if that was taken out, but there was no answer. After a while it was decided to leave it to anyone who would volunteer, needless to say it was left to the teachers with a religious background.

My daughter Karen with her son, my grandson David, came with my Mother for a couple of week's holiday and we did exactly the same as when my other daughter Michelle came. They said it was a wonderful holiday and Karen was concerned that I might decide to retire there, but I told her I wished I was going back home with her as my homesickness had started again. It always took a couple of weeks to get over this sickness or depression as I called it. To make matters worse one of my students was found murdered, she had also been molested. It was the first murder to happen on the island and it caused a lot of anxiety, but they caught the man responsible. Then one of the boys, named Brandy, who had been expelled was found dead not far away from the school in a gulley. They said it was connected with drugs. I'm afraid the modern world was spreading to Nevis and it needed more Police. There were only two men and one lady for the whole island, this I mentioned when I was called to speak to the staff. After this the police force was doubled and things calmed down.

Marlene had a message from Head Office saying our director from London was paying a visit and for us to make arrangements, we left it to Marlene as she had Bob's car and could pick up and run them around the island. They had a meeting with the Premier and afterwards arrived at the VTC, I was introduced to David Green, our director, by Marlene.

'Yes, I can see you've done a wonderful project here and everyone I've spoken to has said so,' said David. 'How have things been since Mr Neil died?'

'A few hiccups, but otherwise very good.' I replied.

'Do you think they could manage without VSO support on the island?'

'Yes,' said Pat. 'Since the VTC was finished by Roy, the centre has come on in leaps and bounds.'

'That's correct, there's been a big difference with them taking more responsibility, and I must admit my work has eased off now,' I replied.

'Good, because that is what all the reports I am getting in London say, we in head office are faced with so many requests for personnel, especially from Africa, that we cannot cope, and we have decided not to renew any more VSOs in the West Indies. All our resources will go to Africa this is why I'm here to see whether existing personnel agree. I visited nearly all the VSOs seeking their opinions, mostly all have said the same as you, the most convincing reports come from VSOs who used to teach here and have renewed their contracts and gone to Africa, they are in no doubt that Africa must be our priority, if anyone can give me a better reason I am willing to listen. The Premier has reluctantly agreed but asked if you, Roy, would agree to stay a little more than your contract, to the end of term instead of leaving in the middle, that would lengthen you contract another six months and with your agreement I would allow it.'

'No problem, I would like to go to the graduation?' I replied.

This did not apply to Quinton as he had a work permit and ran the community bee honey company, Marlene was found a position with the government but refused and with sadness quietly left. Pat stayed a couple of months of her own volition, enjoying herself but occasionally popping into her old classroom, all had left except Grant on St Kitts, so I had nowhere to stay the night. I returned the same day on the ferry, Grant had married one of the local teaches and been offered a position teaching English at the local high school.

Pat had been invited by Mr and Mrs Powell who was a local celebrity to a meal at the Golden Rock. I was asked if I would join her.

'Of course' I said, I was always ready for a good meal.

Meeting them was surprising, they were a very old couple, he was eighty years old and she was just a few years younger, he said he was the first coloured man to join the army medical corp.

'Well I never, I too was in the Medics' I said. His eyes lit up, 'I remember a photo of a group in the museum and it said the first Caribbean to join, and you were on it.'

'Yes, that was me, I served in Libya with the eighth army, one of my sons is also in the Medics, he is in your adult class at the VTC. He's building his own house next to mine, we live in the village of Hamilton you are welcome any time.'

'Thank you, I will do that, what is your son's name?'

'David,' he replied.

We had a good meal and there was good conversation, Pam joined us, she told me Michener was still there writing another book, but she did not see him.

'Very rarely comes down for the evening, his wife says he goes into hibernation when he's writing.'

That week I made a point of speaking to the man named David.

'Yes, father said he had a meal with you.'

David was a very quiet man, a policeman on St Kitts but he did not like it to be known. Evidently men on Nevis served on St Kitts and vice versa, this was to avoid familiarity between the population and the law.

'He tells me you were in the Medics.' I said.

'Yes, nine years, started in Queen Elizabeth Barracks, at Aldershot 1958-1969,' he replied.

'Well, well so was I, 1957-1959 National Reserves, I stayed there because I played football for the regiment on the army side,'

'I went to Cyprus and then Germany, you saw my father's picture in the museum,' he said.

'Yes, I replied. 'I think I remember you, in fact I'm sure it was you, I cannot remember any other coloured soldier except RSM Amin, and you're not him.'

He looked at me very strangely.

'Did I ever give you a fortune reading? in those days I would tell them for a bit of extra money.'

'Bloody hell, yes, you came to me at the Sergeant's mess on fatigues, I set you cleaning the tables and although I laughed at you, you were correct in what you said, what a small world.' I said excitedly. 'I'll see you at the weekend.'

David was laying blocks when I arrived, so to his amazement I got my trowel and started to help, we worked until lunch when his wife and Mr Powell shouted us to have something to eat and drink. There were two lads labouring for us, they too were in the police force and they were saying that apart from the drugs and things, St Kitts wasn't all that bad, Nevis was better, but as you know we are not allowed to be police on the same island.'

We had the main meal on Nevis, which is called Goats Water it's like a stew similar to our lobby, it was goats meat and vegetables with a chunk of new bread, washed down with a fruit drink. After that I carried on working until they stopped about 6 o'clock, I didn't like to leave after they had given me my lunch.

Of course this got around that I was helping David and the others would ask if I could help them, it seemed all my adults were building their own houses, some had started to make concrete blocks and were selling them at half the price because they did not have to cover the ferry cost, and Mr Chillington another builder with Blably had bought a concrete lorry for mixing concrete and selling like our ready mix concrete companies.

'Nevis is going to modernise,' they said, laughing.

Great, I thought.

I was sorry to leave Nevis, it was a marvellous two and a half years in which I came to love the island and the people. They gave me a wonderful farewell with presents and speeches, which I will never forget. But Africa was calling.

Tanzania/Kenya/Rwanda

Back at home I decided to spend a few weeks with the family working on the garden and decorating, Karen and Michelle had both re-married. I seemed to be taking the same two down the aisle. When it came to picking a partner my girls couldn't pick their noses. The V.S.O. had accepted my request for a contract in Africa and asked when I would be available. I wanted to go to Australia to see my brother and family for a few weeks. I told them when on return, I would ring them.

Off to Australia I went, calling at Perth to see a childhood friend, Frank Lockett and family for a couple of days. His brother had told him of my arrival and there they were waiting at the airport, and after greeting everyone he drove me to his bungalow by the sea, it was about thirty minutes from the airport. Perth is a very beautiful city, clean but very hot. I told Frank it was lovely, a big difference from Knutton.

'You've done very well, I'm very pleased for you, when you think of the old days when the war was on, you wondered what was to become of us' I said.

'Yes' he said. 'it was difficult for us all but when you think about it we all came out stronger, from what I hear you have all done well except for your wife dying, Florence and I were very sorry when we heard.'

With my air ticket was a promotion offering two free flights in Australia so I used one to fly to Adelaide. Frank took me to the airport where we said our farewells and arranged to meet in the U.K. when he came over.

'Perhaps next year' he said.

Barry and Audrey were waiting for me at the airport with their four children, the two boys and the two girls who I had already seen before when Audrey had brought them for a holiday and they had stayed with us.

I had not seen Barry for twenty five years, and the boys not at all, when the boys saw me they were amazed how much alike I was to their father. After all the hugs the girls starting crying because Joyce was not with me, they drove me to their home going the long way around because they wanted to show me the city.

It was very much like Perth everything looked bright and very clean, Para Hills where they lived was about fifteen minutes drive. It was in an estate of mostly all bungalows and nearly all British descendants. Barry had used the £10 passage to Australia which was on offer then and that is why most of the British arriving in Adelaide came to settle there. They made a fuss and made me more than welcome, giving me a wonderful holiday.

Barry is a twin, Brian is the other brother he lives in a village called Audley, but Barry is the one I have always been fond of as he, like me, was a target of abuse from our parents and I am ashamed to say through my frustration sometimes me.

There is a saying 'you always hurt the ones you love' and I am a master at that.

After three weeks they all took me to the airport, saying their farewells and asking Barry when he was coming to the U.K. he just smiled I already knew it would never happen as when he first flew out to Australia he collapsed on the plane and if it was not for the good luck of a doctor sitting next to them he would have died. He was later diagnosed in hospital as having something unbalanced in his inner ear, at that time they could not do anything for him apart from him not flying or being in a compressive room, but Audrey told me he could have an operation now, but he always said no.

Frank was waiting at Perth airport. I had four hours wait for the U.K. Brittania flight so he decided to come and have a chat and drink with me. I felt that he too like Barry and I had the homesick feeling from time to time. I arrived in Manchester where all the children were waiting for me. They had decided to have a day off and then take me into the city for an evening meal, they must have thought I would be starving. On the contrary I was putting on weight I was now four stone heavier I would have to go on a diet, but there was no need, I was going to Africa.

A letter had arrived from the V.S.O. telling me there was an urgent position in Tanzania for a construction teacher with a bricklaying or stone masonry background. O.k I thought that will do for me I thought it was for a one year only contract and then we would see.

Back at Manchester airport, 'Hello, Roy, here again?' the lady said at the desk.

I must have flown around the world eight times. I would soon be growing wings. Changing flights at Heathrow I arrived at Dar Es Salaam the capital of Tanzania, I was being met by Nick Burn the Area manager who had a number of V.S.O's with him. They all knew one another as they had all been on courses and this was their first contract whereas this was my second. We soon got together and settled down in a Salvation Army compound, in chalets, two persons in each. I was sharing with a young medical graduate named Derek, he was going to a hospital in Arusha which was near to Kilimanjaro.

He was very talkative, always asking me questions, sometimes annoying me but I was glad to say I was not showing it. He became very helpful to me. We were here for two weeks attending lessons and seminars, which was okay but we had to learn Kiswahili and this was a nightmare for me I had difficulty speaking English never mind Kiswahili and it was no secret I was bottom of the class. If it was depending on passing an examination I would have been on the next plane out. But for Derek and his patience I would never been able to say sentences in Kiswahili. I was not too bad at the one words like Hodi Hodi Karibu. (may I come in please)

Habari za nyumbani this is a greeting which everybody uses and you answer Njuri which means fine, Asante means thank you. At the time I thought I would never get use to the language but to my amazement after a couple of months I was talking more Kiswahili than English.

There was another time I found very difficult, we were offered a stay with a local family for a couple of days so that we could get used to the conditions that we were likely to come across. I was one who volunteered, I had already seen the poverty that was going on outside the perimeter of the compound and I was to stay with an office manager and his wife who was one of the primary school teachers. Their dwelling place was round-shaped, built of mud and was painted white, there was a door opening but no windows, a perimeter fence was all around with an opening to walk in and out. Inside part of the fence opening was the toilet, with a bucket of water for hand wash only. Inside was a porch or hall with openings to rooms, one being the dining room with a long table, one side a bench seat and on the other side a couple of chairs, there was a sideboard with photographs of the family and some religious ornaments. One of the openings was my bedroom with a bed made of rough timber and a blanket, and one chair to put my suitcase on. There was no electricity or water. Outside was a fire with pots around, I assumed they were for cooking. They could speak

English and part of the exercise was for me to speak Kiswahili which made the children laugh, they were eager to help me and they went out of their way to make me feel at home. I was finding it difficult but because of the way they treated me I could not disappoint them by leaving, so I stayed the two days. Breakfast was an egg and some kind of bread with a mug of *'English tea'* they said proudly. The children with their beautiful big eyes, which they never took off me, said they had already had their breakfast of porridge, it looked like gruel. I ate and drank everything so as not to offend them.

Back at the compound we were asked to describe our two days. They all seemed to have had a great time and enjoyed it. I was puzzled, was I the only one who found it depressing for people to live like this or had I had it too good on Nevis? When it came to my turn I started to say that everything was ok, but stopped and decided to say what I felt, and that I was ashamed of being a European, it was not the starvation that upset me but the conditions in which these people were having to put up with. The couple I was living with both worked hard, a manager, and a school teacher and yet they lived in such bad conditions. My neighbour's pigeons had better housing. I wanted to know why, and I made up my mind to find out, was I the only one to feel this way?

The room went quiet and they all looked shocked. One female teacher who had been teaching Kiswahili clapped her hands. 'Thank you Mr. Smith for a most honest description, you have touched on the fringe of a condition we have in the whole of Africa - corruption.'

Later some of the V.S.O's told me they did not want to upset the staff but after listening to me and the response the staff gave me they realised how wrong they were and it was a good lesson they will carry it with them when they go out to their positions in the country. They knew I was struggling with my Kiswahili lessons and offered me another week at the compound which I took, along with a couple of other girls.

I was later driven to my V.T.C. to a village called Usangi which was about eight hours drive from Dar Es Salaam on a good tarmac road, the problem was when we came off it took two hours on a rough track to Usangi which lay in a valley, one road or track for want of a better name, in and out the same way. If you climbed up the side of the hills you could see Kilimanjaro with a snow capped top, a magnificent sight that looked about ten miles away but was in reality thirty miles away and took about three hours driving on a bad road.

On entering the V.T.C, I was met by the Headmaster Mr. Kadala and his assistant Mr. Mansuet, who was also a construction teacher. I was told that I would be staying with another V.S.O. named John Wilson but he had gone to Nairobi in Kenya for the week and I had to stay in temporary accommodation, which was an old prison, and the cells had been converted into bedsits. This was awful but as there were other teachers in other cells I did not complain. There were only three classrooms and my first project was to build three more, and I had twelve students to do it with. The first room was a carpenter's class and was fitted out with quite good machines and tools, this is where John taught, the other was a mechanical class with steel bars and cutting and welding machines. The third was to be mine, but was also a classroom for other uses as I would be teaching mostly outside and was only to use it when teaching theory. A Swedish V.S.O. named Sven was teaching mechanics, he was in his twenties, very quiet and had a slight stammer but spoke very good English. His Kiswahili was as bad as mine which made me happy. I started to set out the new building using the same drawings as the existing ones. The lads started to dig out with a couple of shovels and picks.

'Are these the only tools we have?' I asked.

'No,' one boy named Robert said. You have to ask permission of Mansuet who has the only key.'

With that I went to the staff room and asked for the keys to the container which held my tools and equipment. No one answered me so I just stood there for a few minutes when at last Mansuet asked why I wanted them.

'To teach the students' I answered.

'Well, I will unlock the container for you.' he said.

Inside was full of tools and equipment for building, all new and never been used.

'How long have these tools been here?' I asked.

'About one year,' I was told.

'And they have not been used, what have you been teaching with all this time?' I asked.

He just shrugged his shoulders.

'Right boys' I shouted, come and get shovels, picks, lines and peg levels and stuff.'

'Oh Mr. Smith you cannot do this.' said Mansuet.

'Why' I answered.

'Because Mr. Kadala will not like it,' he replied.

'Right, I'll ask Mr. Kadala,' so off I went to see him.

'Why do you need the extra equipment?' was his stupid question.

'I only have two shovels and one pick between twelve students how can I be expected to teach if we have no tools or equipment, John and Sven have their classes fully equipped, why not the construction class?' I asked.

He said they might be stolen, and he was not responsible for them.

I said. 'Oh sorry, do they not steal from the other classes?'

He did not answer, so I thought I'd better not say any more until I had more facts.

Sven said he had not had any tools stolen, Mr Kadala was a crook all the tools had been donated by his Swedish Government, he had complained to his office but had no reply. I thought I'll wait for John as he should have been back by now it was now two weeks since he went.

Sven told me that John refused to have me living with him as he was living with a local girl and was hoping to marry her, he lived along the valley in a three bedroomed bungalow owned by Kadala who is in some kind of project with him.

When John arrived I asked what was going on.

He said he did not know anything about me arriving here, the V.S.O's must have got it wrong.

I said I would go back to Head Office to get it sorted out. I was not staying in the cells anymore, especially with him living alone in a three bedroomed bungalow.

It did not seem to bother him so the next day I caught the bus that travelled to Dar Es Salaam and returned the next day. I took my suitcase just in case I did not return. Head

Office were very surprised to see me and could not believe what John had said, as the field officer Naangela had been to Usangi and had made all the arrangements. When Naangela came into the office Rick questioned her and she confirmed she had been there. I also complained about no equipment so Rick rang the head office in the government to ask why they had requested Mr Smith to teach at Usangi when it was not ready for him. They said they would look into it and they would ring back the next day. They rang back and said there had been some misunderstanding, everything was now ready and their officer was travelling there tomorrow and would Mr. Smith like to join him to make sure everything was as it should be.

I had a day sightseeing. Dar is like two cities, one for the very rich with their grand villas and swimming pools and golf courses, the other part of the city you could smell, never mind see it. It was poverty at its most extreme, and it made me feel sick. It was worse than Usangi and that was bad enough. I had told Rick what I had heard and before I left he gave me a letter for John and one for Kadala. The government officer was a pleasant middle aged man although it was difficult to say how old these people were, as the life expectancy is only forty five years, they found it impossible for me to be sixty. Back at the V.T.C. the officer went to see Kadala, and I went back to my cell, all the other teachers were excited and wanted to know what had happened, as Kadala was very worried and stayed at the centre the whole three days. That was a record, so they knew something was wrong and John also had been in class all the time, he had never done this before. I told them what I had reported and had returned with an officer who was with Kadala now, there was also a letter from V.S.O. to each of them.

Next morning at assembly there were about one hundred and twenty students mostly girls who attended the classrooms on the other side of the square. They were learning to type, dressmaking with their sewing machines and learning the computers. They very rarely came across to what was called the 'boys classes' they only met at assembly in the morning. Mr Kadala looked annoyed, and was standing by the officer who had arrived back with me, also there was a very old but smart man by the name of Mr. Kipundi he was the first head who had started the centre and had retired a year ago.

Kadala introduced the officer who spoke a few words saying that Mr Kipundi was only here part time to help Mr Kadala as the centre was being upgraded to allow extra students who have been granted fees by the government. I did not know they had to pay tuition fees. After assembly everyone went to their classes, my students stood alongside the new excavation not knowing what to do. I went to John and gave him the letter from Rick not saying a word, then turned to Kadala and gave him the other letter, he also handed the keys to the container and told to me that I was responsible for the things inside. I did not trust him or Mansuet, so I changed the lock I had a good Chad lock in my suitcase. The students were delighted, and I made them understand that I was responsible and if they wanted to borrow any of the tools at the weekends they only had to ask but they were to bring them back by Monday morning which they did and I never had any stolen all the time I was there. Mansuet seemed to only take theory and from what I could see the students just copied what he had written on the board. A picture of a shovel with the name shovel under it and so on, a hammer, level, trowel, after one year they were still learning about tools, that was a disgrace.

I told Mansuet this was not acceptable when the students had left, but he just looked sheepish and said nothing. I had completed the excavation, the lads had done well they had learned to set out with the lines and to square the building using the four three five system that is four foot long one side of the line and three foot along the other and if the lines are square from the end of the three foot mark and the four foot mark should be five foot if not it's not square so I told them to keep adjusting the lines until it is. After this we started to put pegs in the bottom of the trench nine inches high and levelling with a staff about ten foot long to another peg which was knocked in the ground until it was level with the first peg then carry on doing the same until you get all the way round. When this was completed we concreted all the way round to the top of the pegs. This took about three weeks to get to this stage. In the meantime some of the lads had been making concrete blocks in a mould the same as I did in Nevis. There was a lot of stone in the area so I decided to use this to the floor height. While I was supervising all this, Sven had invited me to stay with him in a lovely bungalow half way up the side of the valley. It was much cooler there and pleasant, meanwhile John, who had been told to leave at the end of the month told me I could have the keys to his place but I refused.

I said I was better with Sven if that was alright. He said yes so I told John where to put his keys which upset him and Kadala was also upset because he was receiving money from the government each month for letting to the V.S.O. I did not see John again after he left, but other teachers had told me he and his girlfriend were living in Nairobi, and Mangela was dismissed from the V.S.O. I never found out what was the truth of the matter but you could guess corruption was part of it. Mr. Kipundi was a godsend to me, he was always helping and taking classes when one of the teachers were away. He also took the carpenter's classes as he was a carpenter by trade he told me.

Sven had good news, his boss was calling the next day with a vehicle for him. The V.S.O. had sent a mountain bike for me, how stupid can you get, it was difficult for cars never mind a bike, I ended up giving it to the school for the use of my students and they loved it, and made a rota for the daily use of it. Sven's boss came into the school square driving a four wheeled drive Suzuki with another one behind.

'That's yours' he said, pointing to it and shaking Sven's hand.

'Great' Sven said.

He introduced me to his boss then took him around the centre and asked if he was settling down.

'I had the impression you were not happy the last time I saw you.' he said.

'Yes, it's much better now, things have altered a lot since I saw you last.' Sven replied.

They didn't stay long, and when they left Sven said we would be doing a little sightseeing at weekends.

'Roy, I'll get some maps' he said. I think we will go to the Rift Valley to see the rhinos, another weekend we will go to the Narragora Crater, a phenomenon from millions of years ago where most of the wild animals seem to live.' We were travelling through towns called Moshi and Arusha where most of the tourists prepare themselves for climbing Kilimanjaro. In the week we concentrated on V.T.C. but every weekend we went touring sometimes taking a couple of students.

The centre's new classrooms were up to window height, I made a change in the mortar to lay the stone which was mud or soil mixed with water, the soil had a clay texture therefore making it plyable to cement and sand mortar as the Danish road contractors had donated to the centre a load of sand and a few bags of cement. With more students we were rapidly approaching the roof height where with Mr Kipundi's help we were beginning to take measurements for the construction of the roof, a pitched roof with tin sheets to make it rainproof. The inside we filled in with stone and concreted the floor this was a long process, because the existing floors in the old classrooms were collapsing due to termites eating the soil under the concrete, this is why I pointed out to my students we must fill with stones first. It had taken just over six months to complete to which Mansuet sarcastically said it was the same time it took to build the old one.

'But this one is much better constructed, it will not need new floors and the tin sheets on the roof will stay on.' I said.

We divided it into three classrooms, we white-washed all the walls, put frames in the windows, we tacked mesh on which I had brought from Dar to stop the mosquitos and flies, plastic strips to hang in the doorways, I was not taking any chances as I still needed to take my malaria tablets. I must say I was proud of the students. Now this was completed I wanted to build an extension on one of the old buildings and make it into a canteen. The students to my knowledge had nothing to eat or drink from 7:00am until 5:00pm, I sometimes caught them stripping the outside of the sugar beet and eating the middle part or eating raw corn cobs. I asked Kipundi for permission, he knew I would not ask Kadala, after a couple of days Kipundi said yes, he had talked to the elders and they agreed. In Usangi there were a few shall we say shops and they were all run by Pakistanis, no matter where you go in this world they are there running their little businesses, if you want anything they will get it so I ordered one dozen drawing sets which I had seen in Dar, they had a pencil, ruler, compass, protractor, etc., on a cardboard frame at a cost of nine hundred shillings around one pound in English currency, so it should have come to twelve pounds in English currency, but the Pakistanis charged me fourteen pounds, it was no problem, I suppose they had to make a profit.

I had already given them an exercise book and told them the project was to build a canteen, giving them the sets I told them to draw the plans with the correct measurements and things to arrange inside, and the best one will be selected, you have a week to draw it, the sets are yours so don't lose them. They, like the tools in the container guarded them with their lives.

'We are going to climb Kilimanjaro at the weekend' Sven smiled.

'Oh dear, I'm not as young as I used to be.' I said.

'Two students are going to guide us and they said they will carry you the cheeky gits.' he said.

I managed, but the pain I had in my chest told me to stop smoking, we slept in our sleeping bags as it was very cold but the views were magnificent. The next day coming down was much easier, afterwards we climbed Kilimanjaro a number of times mainly as guides for charities that V.S.O. organised much to the local people's annoyance. We still paid them to accompany us. The V.T.C. and Kadala were always trying to find money or sponsors and on a rare occasion asked if I could organize some way of making money for the centre. The Danish contractors were still sending us a load of sand and cement on occasions, so we could still make concrete blocks and sell them. I had noticed the Pakistani's were having them delivered from Dar.,

'We can make them better and cheaper I told Kadala, but you will have to agree a price as I don't have that information.' His eyes lit up, and in a matter of weeks we could not cope with the orders, whether he made money for himself I don't know, but as long as the centre was prospering I let it go.

Robert won the drawing contest voted by the other students and they started the foundations as I had taught them using the Pythagoras method to square, it was a great delight watching for that was now all I was doing. Sven had in his bungalow a drinking water machine it was like a central heating boiler on the wall as we have back home, only this had two compartments, the top one was to receive hot (boiled) water, in it was what looked like large candle sticks they were hollow and made of ceramic material, the idea was water would filter through them like blotting paper and enter into the bottom chamber where it was refrigerated, we had a generator but with having electricity we did not need it. The village was being supplied with electricity by a company financed by the U.N. It was about time the U.N started to do something even though it's about fifty years late I thought. I had a letter from Nick Burns my boss saying there was an annual Conference at Mombasa and all the V.S.O's must report to head office, a week's leave had been granted by the V.T.C. This I did and had a wonderful week in a hotel by the sea close to Mombasa, not a four star but it was clean and the food was edible although there was too much salad. 'I don't like rabbit food' a V.S.O. named Alan said and I agreed. It was great meeting friends, talking to them, apart from seeing the poverty we were all coping, we had not heard of anyone going back home.

There were a lot of seminars and lectures, one day Lord Carrington gave a speech and stayed a couple of days but he never bought me a pint or invited me onto his yacht.

'Ah' he said, 'so you were one of those invited were you? he said with a smile, V.S.O know everything,' touching his nose.

One thing that upset us was V.S.O. had sent a person to help on the game reserve and quite a few people objected, one said he was working on the outskirts of Dar with the poor, trying to get them medical attention and he had been asking for other doctors to help for twelve months and here we are looking after animals better, he said, everyone stood up and clapped. One lady who was working in the Seringati area said there were four vets but only one doctor in their village. To rub salt in, she said one had been looking after the hounds in Buckinghamshire, we only have two wild animals, the Fox and Badger and we kill them for sport and fun, again everybody stood and clapped. The directors all agreed and promised to make it known in London.

While I was there I befriended Alan the salad man as I called him to his annoyance, he was building and renovating in Zanzibar for the council, he was more like a foreman and he loved it.

'I am staying there, he said they will have to sack me but that will not bother me if they do, other builders have offered me a position with them would you like to come over for a night? I can fix you up its only one hour across on the ferry.'

'Yes, after this finishes I'll go over with you.' I replied.

Saying my good-byes I left with Alan and went across to Zanzibar. It was quite a contrast, it was all stone buildings, that is why the main town is called Stone Town, it is not allowed to build with any other material and colours are not allowed only white. The people you can tell are of Arab descent and years ago were an Arab island ruled by themselves, since the war it has come under the control of Tanzania which they dislike but accept with no bother. I liked Zanzibar but I was glad to return to Usangi.

The students had completed the canteen and Sven had bought and fixed the drinking water machine, electricity was on but not connected which I soon wired up without any difficulty, the next day the students were queuing until it had all gone.

'We will have to get another' I said to Sven, I'll try my V.S.O connections this time, but I've already asked for a cooker, we also need a fridge and sink unit with a tap, that's where Kadala comes in or Manseut plus utensils to cook with.' One of the older students Serena, who was leaving asked if she could run the canteen I told her I didn't see why not but she would have to speak to Kadala or Kipundi which she did and there she was, making cups of tea or coffee and making a kind of pancake with the local honey on and she only charged a small fee which everyone accepted as fine.

After a few weeks I asked Serena how it was going, she said it was difficult making it pay as some children had no money but all were hungry, so what could we do. I asked about this at the next staff meeting, the Domestic Teacher named Hamidah, said she was waiting for an assistant in the kitchen, maybe Serena would accept it on an agreed salary as well as running the canteen with the students using the same principle as Mr Smith uses with his students building at the same time teaching. This was agreed and Serena accepted, this relieved the finances and the money raised went all on the food supply. After a word with the Pakistani's who wished to be part of the community, food was supplied at a good rate, this was a success but made our extension for the kitchen too small. The next project was to extend, again the students got their drawing pads out and made a start. At this time I became aware of some students who were sleeping at night in the classrooms. I asked why, and they said because it was better than nyumbani (home). Others had to walk or run six miles to school and six miles back and sometimes were too tired to do anything. Ever likely they win all the gold medals in the Olympics I thought. This started me to think about building a dormitory. I talked about this to Sven and Kipundi. They agreed and Mr. Kipundi said that he knew of such a place already at a school in the next village called Mwenza about one hour's drive away. Sven said he would drive us there the next day. Kipundi asked if Kadala could come also, we said yes, perhaps it was time to mend fences. After we had been given permission from the Headmaster who knew Kipundi, we walked around the dormitory it was about the same size as our classrooms, but with more windows and at a higher level to stop people looking in.

Inside, some students were lying on their beds reading or writing, as this was Saturday, a free day. There were ten beds each side of the room and at the end an opening leading to the toilets and wash basins and showers, outside I noticed a septic tank cover.

'This is what we would have to build, I said and my boys can make beds better than these wooden ones, in angle iron.'

'Mr Kipundi can make timber slots' said Sven. Kipundi nodded.

'We can also make a cabinet for each bed like those,' he pointed out.

'It is a good project, do you think we can do it, what about the finances?' said Kadala.

Kapundi said 'we thought we would get sponsors, it will be possible with Mr Smith's and Mr Jonson's contacts.'

On Sunday, Sven and I went for the day to Kilimanjaro but we did no climbing and stopped at the Masa Mora game reserve. The local Masi had a market open, so Sven and I walked around. I did not like the Masi, I thought they were an idle, arrogant, miserable lot, and did nothing in the community to make things better, they just stood on the spot jumping up and down.

'What do they do that for?' I asked Sven.

'Oh it helps them to grow tall' he said laughing.

Some Masi looking at us did not like to see us laughing and seemed to be surrounding us, when an old man shouted at them and they moved away. He then stared at us with an angry look on his face so I said 'it's time we moved.' Sven agreed.

We went on back to Usangi where we were met by Kadala, a driver had delivered two letters, one for me and one for him from the V.S.O the letter said that I was to go to Mwenza where I would be picked up by the U.N. vehicles who were on their way to the Rwandan border to build a refugee camp. We were asked to take our portable toilets and extra clothes as we may be asked to stay for a few weeks.

Rwanda

Rwanda was the last contract for V.S.O in which I was personally involved, it introduced me to events which I would never wish to see again. At this time I was working on a refugee camp on the Tanzania side of the border supervising the construction of tents and canvas areas to accommodate the refugee clinics with clean water and septic tanks for ablutions and toiletries. One morning a group were going across the border to see what was going on as we had heard of terrible things and it was here I saw the results of some of the most dreadful atrocious inflicted on human beings.

Firstly, we all saw the terrible results of a massacre of men, women and children who had sought refuge in a church, a place that should have been their sanctuary. Apparently these people were advised by the religious authorities to go, this proved fatal and I believe the ministers abandoned them. We counted one hundred and sixty skeletons of victims who had been savagely slaughtered. Although the world press had made it four hundred I failed to find out where they got their information from. You can Imagine my feelings of anger, sadness and a developing doubt about the existence of God. How could human beings irrespective of their religion whether Christian or Muslim do that to other humans. In this terrible situation I noticed a group of children close by, it didn't take a genius to see that they were the victims of malnutrition.

At this time I was a very heavy smoker and I reckon that I smoked close on sixty cigarettes a day, unknowingly I had dropped a packet of cigarettes, what I next saw affected me terribly, I saw the children grab the cigarettes, thinking to myself they were going to smoke them, but to my horror they were so desperate for food they were eating them. This affected me so much I never smoked another cigarette after that. Seeing people today smoking gives me flashbacks, I think what a lot of money we spend on cigarettes and the money would help their plight.

Returning to Tanzania, I enquired about the ministers in the camp, there were a few there but most of them had left, it was a good job because of the way I was feeling at the time. Three of the girls helping out were Irish second trip nurses, and they intended to pursue this all the way to the Vatican, but to no avail.

I only went back to Rwanda one more time and that was to help Miss Diane Fossey who had arrived at the camp asking for assistance in looking for some gorillas. I realised she was the lady I had seen on the television looking after the gorillas in Uganda. She was a very brave lady, I don't think I could do what she has done so without hesitation I volunteered with the others. We spent all day searching and questioning the local people who were of no help. She found the area where the gorillas played and ate. Diane knew that they had been there, we both thought they had gone the same way as my cigarettes.

Jeanne, one of the nurses who was with me at the chapel rings me from time to time especially at Christmas, she is still trying to get answers, I think she would have made a very good nun as she seems to have a very strong religious manner.

Back at the refugee camp things were improving, some of them had gone to try to find friends and relatives although it was against our wishes. The fighting had died down in the last two days, although around two hundred and sixty people had died and we were only one camp of many. I had been there about six weeks and the medical staff had put a rota up for us to have a few days away from the camp. I decided to have mine and go to Usangi and catch up with the students to see how they were coping. They were delighted to see me and looked and talked to me as though I had never been away.

Sven and Kipundi said I looked ill and thought I had lost weight, I was not eating much and had very little sleep I was tired all the time and had very little energy.

The extra kitchen extension was nearly ready and the foundations were in for the dormitory, I told my students they had done very well and congratulated them.

'Mr Mansuet has helped us,' said Josef, eagerly waiting to see or hear what I'd say about that.

'How did you find him?' I replied.

'He is okay now', said Freddy.

'But not as good as you Mr Roy' said Robert.

'Give that man a sweet' I said, and we all laughed.

Sven was worried, I could tell how he kept looking at me and putting extra food on my plate. At night we would go to the village and have a beer, Tanzania brew which was called Safari, forty pence a bottle in English money, it was a weak kind of lager but I enjoyed it and the company. The local men of the village told us if you go over the border into Kenya the village there sell Tusker beer a Kenyon brew, it was much better and stronger but it was sixty pence a pint. One night Sven drove us over and we had a few bottles, yes they were right, it was much better.

'We will take a few home with us' said Sven this we did, and on our way back in the middle of the track were three lions.

'Bloody hell, stop' I shouted.

'No way' said Sven and swerved around them in a low gear making as much noise as possible, this scared them away.

'Now you know why we don't walk over' said one of the locals.

The next day there was a commotion in the village, two Masi men had been attacked by a pride of lions, they were being carried in a blanket by four men at each corner, to the local hospital. I called it a clinic and that was over stating it with a doctor attending every other day. 'Hope he's here today' I said. One of the female teachers said she was going to see if she could help, and asked if I would join her as she knew I had first aid knowledge, so off we went to the clinic. As luck happened, the doctor was there, a Tanzanian, who spoke good English. I asked if there was anything I could do.

'Yes, he said, help me to put stitches in these wounds while I try and stop the bleeding.'

I went to go and help when the doctor said.

'Not him, he's dead, he's lost too much blood but this one has a chance.'

I put a tourniquet around his left leg at the groin height which stopped the blood and I started to put glip stitches down the badly cut leg, squeezing the flesh the best I could. The female teacher was cleaning away the surplus blood and trying to hold the flesh close together for me. We did the same on his arm the doctor was working on his neck.

'There's an artery damaged, I'm having difficulty repairing it, the others are okay now but this one keeps leaking, can you hold it while I slip a stent in, that's the only thing I can do?'

Hamidah released the tourniquets for a few minutes and then tightened them again.

'Good, that has done the trick, you can release now, he said to me, thank you both for your help.'

The doctor said he knew Hamidah did a little nursing and he had noticed that on my C.V. I had been in the army medical corp. He told me he was one of the elders who had asked for me when he read my C.V, he also asked me if I had been on the Rwandan border. I told him I had been there for six weeks. He asked how I was health wise, I told him I had not been very well and had lost a lot of energy and he said he would have a look at me as soon as he had given the sick man his blood transfusion.

'How do you think the lad will go on?' I asked.

'It's less than fifty-fifty I'm afraid.'

He put the blood drip on and also a saline one. I was surprised that he had all this equipment but he said it was the building that he needed as the old ward had been here before he was born he was hoping that the students would build one like the dormitory I was building. I said I would put it on the project list and get the students to draw up the plans as it would be a good exercise for them.

He told me to hold up my arm as he wanted to check my blood pressure. He said it was high, much too high and he needed to hear my chest. He went round the back and then the front and then back again. He said something did not sound right and had I noticed a change in my breathing. I said it may have something to do with me not smoking as I had given up about a month before. I asked him could it be withdrawal symptoms. He told me the next time I was in Dar I was to go to the hospital for some test and he would give me a letter and I was to go to the embassy's hospital which was better even if I had to pay, the V.S.O would reimburse me.

I had noticed that since I came back from Rwanda that Mansuet, if he did not have a class, would sit at the back listening to me. At first I did not like it, it made me feel uncomfortable but I thought what the hell, as long as he does not interfere. At one lesson I was teaching how to read a plan with no measurements on it.

'That's impossible' Josef said.

'No I answered, we call it a plan to scale, say half an inch to 1 yard. I told them there can be many scales but I would teach them the above. If they had a line on their drawing that measured six inches using the scale above, how long would it be in a practicable sight measurement? The lads look puzzled, so I left them while I had a cup of coffee with Serena. When I got back, the boys all had different answers, but no one was correct. The answers ranged from six yards to sixty yards. I asked them how many halves there were in six inches, after a while they all agreed on twelve so I asked them what did the scale half inch represent they all replied one yard. I could see Robert was making a table but doing it the long way round but he had got the idea, some of the others also shouted twelve yards at last they had got it and if there were no measurements on some of the drawings the scale rule was applied using many other numbers and scales. The students in their eagerness had got it. Mansuet came to me after the lesson and told me that John had never taught him that when he was a student. This surprised me and I asked if he went to school in Dar to be a teacher. He told me this was the only school he had ever attended he told me it was John who recommended him to teach here. This threw a different light on my opinion of him as he was only teaching what John had taught him and that was nothing and it made Kadala easy to control him.

Gradually I bought him to be more involved with lessons, showing him ways and giving him more confidence and it was beginning to pay off. Kadala was more noticeably around school showing an interest. The school had doubled in size and the number of students had trebled making it the largest and best V.T.C in Tanzania, as he quite often said to visitors. As the weeks went by I seemed to be getting worse health wise and one day, feeling pretty low I said aloud 'what the bloody hell am I doing here, feeling so ill.'

The students all looked up at me in surprise and then Robert said.

'Because God has sent you to help us.'

I didn't know whether to laugh or cry, how could I tell him I was an atheist. Before I went to Rwanda I was already a doubting Thomas and after that it was the end of my faith in religion but for some unknown reason I hated the word atheist. How could I answer Robert and the other students, it was the only hope they had. Every Sunday, dressed in their only clothes that they had carefully washed and ironed they flooded to all the local churches to pray.

'Yes' I said to Robert smiling, they are all happy, why should I upset them they will learn as they grow up one way or another.

Sven said that one weekend he would like to go to Dar to the head office, I said I would like to go too. When we got there we said 'hodi, hodi' to the girls that were sitting at their desks, looking up they replied, 'asante habori nzuri.'

Nick came into the office and asked me how I was feeling, I told him I was not too well. Nick said that he could see that Rwanda and the refugee camp were pretty bad as the girls had told him about it. I told him that is why I had come to Dar as I had been putting it off for weeks hoping it would wear off but it had not. I told Nick that the local doctor had given me a letter for the hospital and could he arrange for me to go to the one at the embassy. He told me he could take me straight away and we had a quick coffee and went to the hospital. He had a lot to say as we drove there as I had been busy with the school and he was also busy with requests for personnel. He told me that good staff was hard to get as I had found out with Naangela. He asked me if I knew she had two jobs, and was not looking after me and other V.S.O's personal requests, and she had the cheek when found out to hand in her notice.

At the hospital the receptionist asked us to sit and wait while she phoned for a doctor who came after a ten minute wait. I gave him the letter and he told me I would require an X RAY and then an E.C.G. After about one hour the diagnosis was that the angiograph showed as least three blockages and they recommended me to go home and have further tests. Nick told me it was better to go home to have any operation I might need. I told him I needed at least a couple of weeks to prepare my students and the centre. I asked him if they had got a replacement for me but not to get another John. Nick said he would put the wheels in motion for somebody to take over and when they decided they would let me have the final say.

On the way back to Usangi I told Sven and told him not to keep it a secret. If people asked he was to tell them that I would be leaving but I was hoping to return when my health had improved. The village soon knew, the jungle drums saw to that, they all wished me well and hoped that I would return. The last few weeks I pushed Mansuet very hard until he became a good teacher. I told him so and he seemed very grateful. I told him he had a one sided opinion when I first arrived, but I too had the same opinion about him which in hindsight I should have known better as it is better to listen to both sides and then give your opinion. I told him all this hoping it would help him when my replacement arrived. My good friend Sven drove me to my head office in Dar, we said our farewells, exchanged addresses and phone numbers and we said we would hope to meet again. Later Nick drove me to the airport and I was back on my way home to Blighty.

End of Overseas Work for V. S. O

Arriving home from Africa, I had a medical at the V.S.O hospital for tropical diseases in Putney, London. They told me that as far as diseases go I had passed, but that I should see my own doctor in regard to my other complaints. This I did, and he sent me to a consultant at my local hospital, The North Staffordshire Royal Infirmary. After giving me an examination and reading my letter from the doctors in Dar he said he agreed with everything in the letter but he would like me to have an angiograph to see exactly where the blockage was. He and another doctor threaded a wire from my groin towards my heart, I was able to see it travelling up on the monitor and then it stopped. They kept trying but there was no way through. They had to try another way but the same thing happened and then they tried a third way without success.

'Mr Smith, I'm afraid it is a triple bypass for you, I'll speak to the surgeon and let you know in a day or two' said the doctor.

Mr Abid was the surgeon and when he interviewed me he told me it was definitely a triple and at the same time he was to check on a value. He told me there was nothing to worry about as he had done many bypasses without any difficulty.

'I hope they are better than the bypasses I have worked on' I said.

His eyes lit up.

'What do you mean?' he replied.

I told him I had worked on the Chester, Nantwich, St. Asaph and the Lime Kiln Hanley to Bucknall bypasses.

He smiled and said he travelled through Lime Kiln bank every day and he could guarantee his were better than mine. He always calls me the engineer when he sees me now.

Having the operation was no problem to me but afterwards it was very painful, my chest had been opened and stitched back from my neck to my belly button. My legs were bandaged where they had taken my veins out to use for the operation.

'We thought we had lost you Mr Smith but you are going to be fine.' Said the doctor, reassuring me.

I looked around the ward, seeking something to recognise to assure myself as to whether I was alive or was this the afterlife. 'Bloody idiot' I told myself, I must be going mad.

'Hello engineer, Mr Abid said, how do you feel?'

I told him it hurt when I swallowed and it was even worse when I coughed. He told me that would eventually pass but he told me that I had had five bypasses and that the value was cleaned and blood and built up on the side because of the lack of a good flow. I asked him was that a record having five bypasses, he told me that the most you could have was seven.

He came to see me every day and on the sixth day he told me I could go home.

I phoned my daughter and she came to collect me. When she saw me she fainted, and the nurses had to look after her. We all laughed, and she never lived it down. She told me I looked so ill and I said I was in terrible pain and the pain killers were not helping but the doctor did not want me to have Warfarine, he said I could get addicted so I was to try and persevere. I had known a few old friends, well, I thought they were friends, who had had this operation and they said there was no pain at all and it was the best thing they had ever had done and now they are all as fit as a fiddle. 'I'll fiddle them next time I see them' I thought.

It was about six weeks later and things were much better when, at a football meeting for old players I saw Tony, one of those who told me that he had no problem after his operation. When he saw me his head went down but there was a big smile on his face. I told him what I thought and was he sure he had had a bypass. He replied that he had had a triple bypass but if he had told me the truth I would never have had it done.

'Too bloody true, I said, but I'm getting better.'

'There you are, he said, in a couple of years you'll be as fit as me.'

'Two years? Don't say anymore, just get me a pint.' I said.

The VSO kept in touch either by phone or letter always wanting me to go to Mongolia or Kilimanjaro for some charity event. One thing I do enjoy is going to Howarth Hall in Birmingham to answer questions from students about countries that I have been to and where they are going to, questions like shall I take this or that or is it okay to do such a thing. I try to be as honest as I can because I know how desperate the young students need them, but the conditions and to see the poverty might put them off so I gently put it to them that things are very different over there.

Wynn Jones is a name that keeps popping up. I remember it being the ambassador's family name in Cuba also the officer's name who was the equerry to Prince Philip that invited us onto the Royal Yacht for cocktails and to watch the band play the retreat. To my amazement, years later Wynn Jones was the sole survivor in the car crash that killed Princess Diana. I thought it was an amazing coincidence, but I suppose my training in remembering things, places and people while in the army comes naturally to me. Perhaps readers may begin to think there is a little more to my overseas adventures than meets the eye.

My training in Holland may not be all about building slaughter factories in Cuba, as there was a lot going on in

Cuba that people were eager to know or working in Libya may not only be to construct airfields. Libya was beginning to be a problem, and information was widely sort after. Gaining the trust of Arabs was also an advantage. Where was all the money coming from to buy one of the major stores in London or hotels on Park Lane? They had properties all around, was the money coming from gun runners? Defence was a lucrative business to be in, supplying aircraft and so on.

Was the PM's son a major player, was there more to building a hotel in Jordan on the Israeli border, what was the problem on the west bank and what part were the PLO playing? Again information was desperately wanted. I needed a position with less aggravation after my bereavement and accepted the VSO position but once again was there another side as on St. Kitts and Nevis there lived a lot of wealthy, powerful people. Money laundering and drugs were rife. What about poor old Africa, where was all the money from governments all over the world in grants going? The millions given by charities certainly did not go to where it was intended. I must admit a water tap was supplied only to the odd village, it's about time money was stopped and food and materials were supplied instead. I am told the Swiss banks are full of charities money. Maybe my next position will be in Switzerland but I'm not holding my breath.